Exploring Corporate Shared Values

Alex Ndukwe

First printing, 2020

Printed in the united states of America

ISBN: 978-1-67811-027-7

Dedication

This book is dedicated to Chukwuma Ojei, CEO of Prince Ebeano Supermarket for their CSR initiatives that have affected communities nationwide.

Table of contents

Exploring Shared Value

Origin of Shared Value

Corporate social responsibility (CSR) has been a very popular concept with respect to corporate institutions, Religious bodies and the reasons are not farfetched because they want to give back to society. The question is at what cost? And how can the drive be sustained considering the availability of funds?

The new world order is the shared-Values that would replace the CSR, around the world the concept is been embraced and implemented by some corporations. This concept is not one-sided but a win-win situation, social needs unveils Business opportunity, deploying corporate Assets and expertise leads to meeting the social needs and impacting on the bottom line of the corporation in terms of profitability. This ensures that the needs are met in our society on a permanent basis while business is in progress.

Exploring Shared Value

Government around the world are faced with scarce resource and providing infrastructures becomes a challenge, the only option available at their disposal is to borrow from the IMF, World Bank, Lending clubs. Unfortunately, in Africa such facilities flow into the pockets of those at the hem of affairs, poverty is unleashed in Africa but if this concept can be embraced the pressure on borrowing will be eliminated.

Porter and Kramer (2011) define the shared value creation as "... policies and operating practices that enhance the competitiveness of a company as well as the economic and social conditions in the communities in which it operates." (p.6). The authors argue that the CSV is the next step the classic social responsibility should take, which is criticized as being an attempt of companies to generate a good image, but that does not necessarily produce strategic benefits to organizations. Creating shared value then seeks to fill the existing gap of

Exploring Shared Value

how to generate economic value for the company (Maltz, Thompson, & Ringold, 2011) while value to society is given (Pirson, 2012) from activities of social responsibility with a strategic approach. (1)

You must have come across the term, 'Creating shared value', this is basically the same but could be used and described James Epstein-Reeves on Forbes.

What does the term "creating shared value" mean? It already has an acronym, CSV, and it's, in fact, a powerful concept for companies to use. Ultimately, it's a strategy for developing the future market while also strengthening economies, the marketplace, communities, and corporate coffers. But the term runs the risk of being confused with the phrase "corporate social responsibility (CSR)" or, worse, with the idea of redistributing wealth. To combat the confusion, we are launching a video to illustrate and explain the concept of CSV.

Exploring Shared Value

Chapter 1

Share value vs CSR

The CSR could be described as affecting lives positively without any profit, apart from profit most organisations describe it as giving back to the society and it is usually executed once a year as a parting gift for that trading financial year.

Interestingly religious organisations have embraced this concept as a welfare initiative by feeding less privileged, building hospitals, schools etc. , the challenge is that CSR only meets the immediate needs and doesn't really eradicate social problems as identified in the society.

We believe that CSR is different—if overlapping—a concept from creating shared value. Corporate social responsibility is widely perceived as a cost centre, not a profit centre. In contrast, shared value creation is about new business opportunities that create new markets, improve profitability and strengthen competitive positioning. CSR is about responsibility; CSV is about creating value. Certainly, the phrase "doing well by doing good" covers both shared value initiatives like the Chevy Volt—a new product we see as shared value—and more traditional CSR activities such as GRI reporting that responsible companies accept as a cost of doing business. But they represent very different strategic and management decisions.

(CSR vs. CSV - What's the difference? Mark Kramer, Remaining Social Change Blog)

There are tendencies that the CSR and CSV can overlap, this means it could address a social need that will improve the quality of life and still rub on the needs of the business, let me give an example, recently Prince Ebano Supermarket constructed a 3.7km road from Gudu to Lokogoma in Abuja and this road leads to the environment where there Store is located, this ought to be a CSR initiative but it's beyond that because the same road has a bridge that has taken the lives of some citizens, government had awarded the project and the contractor had not been mobilized, the corporate body took up the responsibility and this road has eased the traffic on Apo-Shoprite road. I see this as a CSR turned shared value because a challenge had been resolved that will impact on real estate owners on that road, it will also boost the customer base of that supermarket, in logical terms we cannot give projection of the profit at this time, emotionally this feat has advertised prince ebeano, most people in the environment ask questions and the statement that emanates is "I must patronize that supermarket".

CSR is described as a cost centre, you would also realise that this concept could lead to the realisation of projects in our communities and management of this facility would definitely become an issue because funds are not generated from this projects after commissioning and it leads to decay and the donors would have to start all over by planning a renovation that would cost more money.

Exploring Shared Value

One challenge we face in Africa is corruption, corporations provide and delivers projects in the rural communities, it turns out to become a means of livelihood for the chiefs and traditional rulers, funds meant for the sustenance, management of such facility is siphoned.

On the other hand, CSV takes cognisance of needs in the society, though some commentators argue that profits should not be the only focus but ensuring that certain indices are maintained such as culture, pains in such environments are alleviated and the corporations involved make an earning from the efforts that will impact positively on their bottom-line and the societal challenge is resolved for life.

What do you think with respect to underdevelopment in Africa? , this concept will lift the poverty level in our continent if embraced and executed, corporations would resolve societal issues and make an earning and also use such projects to negotiate taxes with their respective governments. This will eradicate the borrowing from world bank et al, the loans are usually embezzled and thereby inflicting pain on generations unborn.

Though we are going to review some case studies with respect to shared value with respect to corporations that have adopted and embraced this concept around the world, one example is Friesland Campina Hong Kong Limited, For over 70 years have been selling dairy in this Asian metropolis. They executed a CSV initiative that helped in preserving the milk tea culture that is fading away, this led to the **training of youths** that are unemployed, they involved restaurants to design the curriculum, this implies that they also created business for them as well, Tea shops were created for students after training and their 'Black & White' milk brand were used at all these outlets. Can we look at the gains of these initiatives:

1) Youths were engaged
2) Employment created

3) Restaurants were involved in this programme

4) Tea shops emerged

5) Milk tea culture preserved

6) 'Black & White' milk became the main component for production

7) Sales of 'Black & White' milk increased

8) Profits generated from this exercise

CSV must be well crafted, considering some issues and most importantly cost-benefit analysis carried out before obtaining Executive management buy-in and without this, it would become difficult to sell the idea.

CSV initiative can **inspire**, **Empower**, **Convene** and **transform** our societies. These are considered as 4 pillars of CSV and we will have to throw more light on them, and they are as follows:

a) **Inspire** – Businesses are challenged to invent new ways of running profitable organisations by aligning profit and purpose, identifying societal issues in their environments, matching it with expertise is the way forward for business to build legitimacy and future-proof their organisation. To inspire the change, a business case should be crafted for shared value and shine the spotlight on alternatives and innovative paths for profit-making.

b) **Empower** - Once inspiration is sparked, inventing new models becomes the next agenda. There should be a connection between daily work and the major challenges we face in our immediate environment or societies. Wherever we sit in an organisation, we can have a positive impact on society while creating value for the company. These issues should be identified with relevant statistical data for a better understanding and by focussing on the business angle, tools should be adopted to identify gaps in the market and do what business does best: solve problems profitably.

c) **Convene** - We recognise that the issues facing us as a society are too large for any corporation to handle alone. It will be wise to build a network that cuts across various sectors of the economy, convene partners from across sectors to share expertise during roundtables and together, identify, implement and scale new solutions. Government, academia, NGOs, social innovation, and of course business, This will also help in identifying challenges easily, build profitable solutions addressing the root of the issues, scale the impact, and eventually build trust with the wider community.

d) **Transform** - The ultimate goal is to change mindsets about the positive impact the private sector can have on challenges that traditionally were left for civil society to deal with or fell in the "too hard basket". Applying CSV principles can help the private sector innovate with strong business models to future-proof their organisations while creating a competitive advantage. In any case, CSV is not easy to achieve and make laudable achievements by co-chairing task forces on each initiative, the need to keep the momentum going on the societal issues and craft solutions to tackle such issues. Shared value journey could inspire employees to invent new ways of doing business, transform their organisations, they recognise the need for change by empowering their staff and collaborating across sectors. Four pillars are built to nudge the private sector toward a different way of doing business, aligning profit and purpose and eventually building trust and relevance in the community.

It is evident that CSV is very thorough compared to CSR, apart from required expertise there is need to collaborate with all the sectors so as a achieve the set objectives, the question here is who will coordinate this Four pillars? , CSV associations have emerged in the advanced societies thereby coordinating these pillars that we have discussed. The associations are visible in all the continents of the world, FSG has been in the forefront by powering Shared Value initiatives.

The essence of this association is to organise training, seminars, a workshop for corporate entities that are members. SV initiative is visible in most countries and it would interest you that they have data with respect to countries, an example is the SV initiative Africa, look at information published in their public domain about Nigeria and Gabon:

The continent offers opportunities beyond natural resources, land and labour-power. We do not have to dig too deep to see that there are a lot of "fast-expanding markets" and pockets of excellence within the continent.

One such opportunity comes from the retail sector. According to a recent report, several countries represent a vast market space for retail. In Gabon, for example, the report suggests that with a GDP per capita of $21,600, the country's newly formed middle class offers significant opportunities to foreign companies, particularly as the domestic retail sector is highly fragmented. Smaller nations such as Botswana and Angola are also offering more and more opportunities. This story also pans out on a larger scale. Nigeria, with a population of 178 million, has a somewhat underdeveloped retail sector. According to the report, modern supermarkets made up only 1% of all shopping expenditure as the market remains dominated by informal shops and convenience stores. Another source of opportunity for foreign businesses comes from the way that cultures and habits are changing. The exceptional economic growth of Nigeria, for example, has allowed for greater consumption, especially for status symbols and products that symbolise "tickets to middle-class membership".

(Creating shared value in Africa is now happening, Mark Esposito, Professor at Harvard University Extension, April 23rd, 2016)

Exploring Shared Value

FSG – is the brain behind the Shared initiative with the aim of impacting the world positively. FSG was founded in 2000 by Harvard Business School Professor Michael E. Porter and Mark Kramer to help foundations create more effective strategies and impact beyond their grant dollars. Today, we are a global firm of 160 people in 6 offices on 3 continents. Each year we use our expertise in strategic planning, implementation, and evaluation to help hundreds of clients such as the Robert Wood Johnson Foundation, Eli Lilly and Company, and Save the Children improve their work in areas that range from health to economic development to education, and more.

Above all else, we believe that real change is possible, that tomorrow doesn't have to be like today, and that passionate people infused with new insights and heightened aspirations can work together to transform our world.

Africa would have to rise and embrace this concept at all levels like corporate entities, public sector institutions. There should be a handshake to actualize the dream of shared value by ensuring that events organised by shared initiative organizations are taken seriously because desired skills that will drive the initiatives can be derived from programs organised.

In Africa we need to focus on the rural areas, these are where food is produced, the initiative should be taken to such communities so as to boost production, adopt technologies that would eliminate waste of produce, this will lift Africa out of poverty and create opportunities for the dwellers, the corporations will be impacted positively while resolving issues at these localities. I quite agree that issues in these communities are overwhelming and the business entities must have a sound knowledge and data to support the needs in these communities.

Corporate bodies should have a dedicated unit or department to carry out this initiative and ensure they leverage the identified issues in their environments, ensure they get management buy-in and above all to ensure that their expertise is brought into play, a win-win situation is derived.

THREE LEVELS OF SHARED VALUE

What does shared value look like? , this will throw more light on this concept.

#1 **Reconceiving Products and Markets**

Meeting societal needs through products and addressing unserved or underserved customers, **Novartis**: To reach customers without health access in rural India, Novartis offers a portfolio of affordable and appropriate medicines tailored to common regional health issues, which is increasing regional sales and doctor visits.

#2 **Redefining Productivity in the Value Chain**

Changing practices in the value chain to drive productivity through better-utilizing resources, employees, and business partners. **Walmart**: By reducing packaging and improving delivery logistics, Walmart saved $200M in distribution costs while growing the quantities being shipped.

#3 Enabling Local Cluster Development

Improving the available skills, supplier base, and supporting institutions in the communities where a company operates to boost productivity, innovation, and growth. **Chevron**: To build prosperity in the region and improve its operating environment, Chevron's "Partner Initiatives in the Niger Delta" uses a data-driven approach to identify new market opportunities and local solutions to unemployment in the region.

In the next chapter, we will take a critical look at case studies drawn from different sectors and impacts derived vis-a-vis profits generated by the corporations involved.

Exploring Shared Value

Chapter 2

Shared Value: Case Studies

This chapter would afford us the opportunity to review case studies and look at ways some cooperation have adopted this concept and impacts derived in our communities, societies at large. We will pick examples from all the sectors of the economy around the globe.

Case Study 1: Friesland Campina Hong Kong: Keeping Traditions with a Visionary Approach

Issue: Much ado about Hong Kong-style Milk Tea, Cha chaan tengs tea culture gradually fading away.

Cha chaan tengs, Hong Kong's version of local cafés, have been an integral part of the city's culture since the 1940s. Originally created as an inexpensive, filling, fast-paced hybrid of local and Western cuisines, the no-frills venues are now an integral part of the city's daily life and collective memory. They've also been responsible for a unique "only in Hong Kong" food culture that has evolved over generations, involving highly specialised techniques requiring training and know-how.

One of the core components of this cuisine is Hong Kong-style milk tea, which has been recognised as one of the20 items that are officially on the first-ever Representative List of Intangible Cultural Heritage of Hong Kong. A twist on British tea drinking traditions, the style that began in the 1940s is made from a mixture of different black teas using methods that vary at different cha chaan tengs.

But it's usually always mixed with one kind of evaporated milk: BLACK & WHITE®, the ubiquitous, nearly 80-year-old Friesland Campina brand made of 100% fresh milk from the Netherlands. According to the South China Morning Post, it's estimated that at one citywide cha chaan teng chain alone, more than 10,000 cups of Hong Kong-style milk tea are made daily.

Exploring Shared Value

Yet due to a variety of factors, cha chaan teng culture and traditions have been on the decline over the last several years. These reasons include a lack of formal on-the-job training programme at many venues. Such venues offer specialised cuisine and techniques that elder generations can't pass to a new generation due to a lack of time, resources and impending retirement. There's also the realistic, everyday aspect of the cafés' relentless, bustling pace, which prevents potential new hires from being taken into the fold.

And, in the case of Hong Kong-style milk tea itself, the drink requires special training — like a good barista at a coffee shop — in order to create a satisfying drink for customers which is unique to Hong Kong. All the above means that dedicated time and training is needed so that would-be employees can handle the daily aspects of the job with speed, competence and know-how. Without a formal succession programme, this is rarely happening today.

Exploring Shared Value

As a result, there have been fears that the traditions and techniques used to prepare such foods — especially Hong Kong-style milk tea — will be lost. In a bid to preserve what can be recognised as a highly specialised art form, FCHK has embarked on a series of initiatives.

The Milk Tea Master Training Programme

In Hong Kong, the company has teamed up with NGOs, a chef management school, and several restaurant groups to create a formal "New Generation Milk Tea Master Training Programme" on a yearly basis since 2016. In 2018, organisations involved include the Hong Kong Confederation of Trade Unions Training Center, Baptist Oi Kwan Social Service, Evangelical Lutheran Church Social Service – Hong Kong ("ELCSS-HK"), Hong Kong Women Development Association and Urban Peacemaker Evangelistic Fellowship, as well as Star Chef Management School, Tai Hing Catering Group, Chrisly Café and Swiss Café.

Exploring Shared Value

The programme was started in 2016 to prevent the technique from dying out and in order to bring new, qualified talent to the industry. In 2018, nearly 30 unemployed Hong Kong citizens (aged 18-59) each received 35 hours' worth of training that involved bar operations, food safety and techniques. 75 per cent of those who took part were then offered a 150-hour internship at a real cha chaan teng where they could receive much needed, fast-paced restaurant experience.

In an extension of the programme to pass on this culture and craftsmanship to the next generation, 20 students from a local secondary school were also selected to formally learn about Hong Kong-style milk tea making techniques and career skills in conjunction with the Youth Career Development Service of ELCSS-HK. The owner of Chrisly Café also provided entrepreneurial advice to students.

At the end of their training, the students were able to put their new knowledge to use via

Exploring Shared Value

BLACK & WHITE®Milkteafé, a ten-day pop-up store held by the company in celebration of the 6thMilk Tea Day at Causeway Bay in November 2018. Two teams of students competed to sell the most BLACK & WHITE®combo sets over the course of a weekend. This provided them with much needed entrepreneurial and specialised Hong Kong-style milk tea training, and most importantly, enriched their lives with the opportunity to explore their interests and career aspirations. All proceeds from the event benefitted elderly service development to acknowledge the elderly's contributions to society.

Results

There have been several tangible short- and long-term results generated from FCHK's Hong Kong-style milk tea master training programme.

First, the training programme has equipped the needy and unemployed with vocational skills to rejoin the job market. The selected trainees themselves were offered a salary and letters of employment after completing their internship. Three of the interns were subsequently offered full-time employment at the cha chaan tengs that they interned with. To date, FCHK has trained nearly 150 professional Hong Kong-style milk tea masters.

All students, meanwhile, gained real-life entrepreneurial skills as two teams competed against one another in terms of selling BLACK & WHITE®combos that included Hong Kong-style milk tea made on-site. One student claimed that "the biggest challenge in making milk tea was time management and this programme gave me a practical opportunity to face society." One intern who graduated mentioned that the programme "allowed me to fulfil my dream," while others were grateful for both the opportunities presented and the recognition that they now have a "commitment to passing on this intangible cultural heritage of Hong Kong to the next generation."

That commitment to passing on this valuable cultural heritage may ultimately offer the biggest benefits for both Hong Kong and FCHK. With so many older milk tea "masters" retiring, the skills acquired by ongoing new trainees will enable the cha chaan tengs — and their traditions — to continue well into the future. It also ensures that it's being done the right way, both in terms of food safety and knowledge about how the business aspects of such venues work.

In the long term, such initiatives successfully keep the BLACK & WHITE®brand in the public eye. Currently, BLACK & WHITE®is the most used evaporated milk brand in nearly 80% of the cha chaan tengs in Hong Kong, based on a study conducted by Nielsen in December 2017 on "Brands in Evaporated Milk Category" among cha chaan tengs in Hong Kong. Such a figure helps BLACK & WHITE®maintain its number one share in the evaporated milk segment amongst its market base. The 79-year-old brand is also used in four out of every five cha chaan teng venues in the city.

As newcomers learn that the fragrance, texture and effect of the brand's use make for a better Hong Kong-style milk tea, the company is also creating the impression that its high quality is associated with good food service. In doing so, BLACK & WHITE® becomes the brand to use at public venues and in the home. Associated promotions, such as the internship programme and an annual public "Hong Kong Milk Tea Day", help make BLACK & WHITE® evaporated milk the premiere must-have item in the category.

By supporting its customers and building capacity in the ecosystem – considered to be a cluster development approach, in shared value terms – demand for the BLACK & WHITE® products is perpetuated. Instead of moving only through traditional channels via wholesalers and distributors, this Training Programme creates and builds vital business-to-consumer relationships that extend to public cafés, such as cha chaan tengs and ultimately, daily consumers. As a result, brand recognition increases even more, and that recognition becomes associated with quality. Once that association has been made, customer loyalty — as seen by the recent Nielsen report — ensues.

While brand loyalty has been one result, regional public recognition has been another. Recently, Friesland Campina Hong Kong was named the winner of two awards at the 10th Asia Responsible Enterprise Awards, which honours Asian businesses for championing responsible and sustainable business practices. This included an award for "Social Empowerment", as the company was selected from amongst 200 entrants across 14 countries.

Exploring Shared Value

As FCHK is clearly seeing a relationship between its public programmes, its community engagement and ensuing results, their initiatives are expected to broaden and continue well into the future. What started as an initiative to help a sector of the community, has enabled a company to see lasting, sustainable results. "Moving forward, we will keep our commitment on nourishing the lives of Hong Kong people across all ages," says Natalie Yuen, Associate Director, Corporate Affairs of Friesland Campina Hong Kong.

That commitment has proved to be more than nourishing. In the case of the New Generation Milk Tea Master Training Programme, it's also offering much-needed work to those who need it, **educating future young employees about entrepreneurial skills and helping to ensure that an important aspect of Hong Kong society** – in this case unique cha chaan tengs – thrives well into the future. That's good for Hong Kong, and **it's proven to be extremely beneficial for FCHK.** A major component for the milk tea is the Black&White milk produced by FCMK and this led to the boost of their revenue because of rising demand.

Case Study 2: Nestle Hong Kong – Healthier Kids Programme

Issue: Today, more than 2 billion people in the world are overweight or obese and 800 million are malnourished. To bring our purpose into action, we believe there is a need to help a new generation to adapt healthier eating habit and proper physical activity.

Thus, the company launched the Nestle for Healthier Kids Programme (previously named as Nestle Healthy Kids programme) in 2009, hoping to raise awareness of the importance of good nutrition and an active lifestyle among school-age children around the world. According to the statistics of the Student Health Service of the Department of Health for school year 2016/2017, one in five primary students in Hong Kong were overweight or obese

As we believe education and health should go together, Nestle Hong Kong has supported the health promotion by Centre for Health Education and Health Promotion (CHEP) of The Chinese University of Hong Kong to launch a 3-years Nestle for Healthier Kids programme in 6 primary schools in 2017.

CHEP had collected data through sessions arranged with the schools for a physical fitness test (test) and student health survey (SHS), in which 536 primary four students participated in the SHS. Among those, 300 students were randomly selected to participate in the test and 298 has completed the test, all of them will be followed up in year 2 and 3 programmes.

The programme features a range of interactive teaching methods and educational contents for students, aiming to promote awareness of healthy eating habit and physical activity such as health consultation session and fruit day at school.

The programme also supports educators and families, who are ultimately responsible for educating the children, in the hope that will create environments in which children develop positive attitudes and behaviour towards food choices and physical activity not only in school but also the community they live.

By improving global nutrition through the promotion of greater awareness, improved knowledge and the effective practice of healthy eating and regular physical activity, Nestle Hong Kong hopes to create positive value for both society and our shareholders.

Problem	Social Impact
Children Overweight and Obese	• Improved health • Enhanced nutrition knowledge • Highlighted the importance of physical activity
Innovation	Business Impact
A program that provides school children, caregiver and parents with access to healthy eating habit and physical activity	• The findings from the Programme could enable the company to realize the existing problem and the needs to improve the nutritional quality of the food products.

Exploring Shared Value

Case Study 3: The MASE project, Micro-franchised agricultural service expansion project Cambodia.

Issue: Around the world, farming communities rely on the land to survive. Without the help of modern agricultural techniques, quality inputs, up to date training and market linkages, farmers struggle to provide for their families.

MASE Project

To address the complex causes of poverty faced by Cambodian farmers, and ensure the sustainability of the social impact is created, World Vision has partnered with iDE and Lors Thmey to develop the Micro-Franchised Agricultural Service Expansion (MASE) Project (2016-2017). Adopting a pro-poor market systems approach to agriculture, the MASE project has considered key questions on how economic value or cost savings can be delivered, private sector engagement and the potential to scale.

The farm business advisor model

The goal of this project is to improve farmers' livelihoods through the Farm Business Advisor Model," says Nem Chheco, the MASE Project Manager in the Takeo province of Cambodia.

Chheco works with World Vision's trusted partners, international NGO iDE and their local social enterprise, Lors Thmey. The Farm Business Advisors at the centre of this project are micro-entrepreneurs who work for Lors Thmey. Through the project, World Vision supports Lors Thmey to recruit and train more local entrepreneurs in Takeo to become Farm Business Advisors.

These advisors play a dual role. They help farmers improve their yields by selling agricultural inputs produced by Lors Thmey, like seeds and drip irrigation. They also provide farmers with much needed agricultural technical support to increase production yields.

Exploring Shared Value

Expanding the total pool of economic and social value The MASE project is creating economic value for all stakeholders in the value chain, in a way that also creates value for the household and community by addressing cost constraints and access challenges previously faced. Like the Farm Business Advisors, Lors Thmey plays a vital double role. The social enterprise supplies quality inputs directly to farmers to improve their yield. It also buys a significant portion of the produce from the farmers to sell on the broader market and grow their business.

By improving production techniques and focusing support on clusters of

smallholder farmers, the project is improving yields, produce quality,

sustainability, and efficiencies along the value chain. This creates more value,

increasing the size of the pie available to all market players – including the

farmers themselves, the enterprises that provide farm inputs and services,

and those that aggregate, transport, process, package, and deliver the farm produce to consumers. Like many small-scale farmers around

the world, in the past Krong Thoeun was forced to travel long distances to work as a labourer. The high cost of transport and low income meant that Krong was struggling to provide for his children. After receiving support through the MASE project to buy quality inputs more locally, cucumber farmer Phat Sarun has seen his crop yields and income double in just months. At first, I didn't know about this model, but I discussed it with my family and we started growing cucumbers. As a result, I now earn enough money to support my children with their schooling and to buy food for my family." – Krong, a farmer in Boreicholsar District "With this plantation, I plan to build a new house next year for my family." – Phat, a farmer in Samrong District

Exploring Shared Value

Achievement highlights

Creating market connections Since the partnership began in 2015,

180 farmers have commenced selling to Lors Thmey directly.

Improving productivity

They have produced a total 1,039 tonnes of cucumber, wax gourd and long beans, bitter gourd, chilli, eggplant, sweet pepper, water spinach and mustard greens, generating US$ 228,156 in revenue for farmers.

Increasing profits in the project's first year, Lors Thmey has sold over US$ 258,000 in total revenue from a combination of high-quality farm inputs direct to farmers and high value produce sold directly to local markets, showing a 186 per cent increase in yearly sales. By the end of 2017, the project is on track to increase Lors Thmey's original sales volume by 363 per cent.

Exploring Shared Value

A winning approach

The MASE project creates a 'win-win' situation for all involved, including smallholder farmers, Farm Business Advisors and Lors Thmey. By empowering smallholder farmers in Cambodia, and around the world with the right skills, knowledge and market connections they will be able to create a better future for themselves and their families.

Case Study 4: SHARED VALUE IN BANKING

Opportunity: Many aspects of Australia's social and economic environment are changing. We are experiencing an increasingly ageing population, coupled with substantial medium-term appreciation in capital city housing values.

Many older Australians have a substantial investment in their family home yet a relatively small capacity for income during retirement, which is often limited to pensions, superannuation and voluntary savings. Funding retirement while retaining familiar living standards has become a real social issue; not just for retirees but also for the Government. In addition, there is the issue of intergenerational equity.

Until the launch of the Homesafe Wealth Release® product in 2005, the main avenues for unlocking home equity were by either downsizing (where cash flow is lumpy and "all or nothing", transactional costs are high and there is a social impact from relocating) or by way of a reverse mortgage, (where longevity risk largely remains with the retiree and is experienced through compound interest eroding equity in the home). In some circumstances, a reverse mortgage is a good option, but it brings the uncertainty of not knowing how large the loan will be. The longer a person lives, the bigger the loan gets and the faster it grows, because of compounding interest. With the Homesafe Wealth Release® product, there is no debt to grow.

Exploring Shared Value

The Strategy

Home safe's goal in addressing this increasingly common social issue was to offer an alternative form of equity release providing certainty for the homeowner. Homesafe provides a mechanism to access the wealth tied up in the family home in a safe and secure manner. The equity release product ensures the right of the homeowner to live in the family home is fully protected. Homesafe allows homeowners to access the capital in their home to supplement living standards during retirement, which helps to address the challenge of funding retirement for an ageing population.

Homesafe facilitates the deferred sale of an agreed proportion of the family home. The homeowner sells a percentage of the future sale proceeds of their home in return for an immediate lump sum cash payment of up to $1 million. The homeowner continues to live in the home until they die or decide to sell the property.

Exploring Shared Value

They make no payments, pay no rent and have control over the property. The homeowner remains the legal owner of the property.

On the sale of the property, which is when the homeowner determines, or on their death, Homesafe will receive a percentage of the sale proceeds, and the homeowner retains the balance. This provides the homeowner with the peace of mind that they will always retain their percentage of the value of their home, not sold to Homesafe. The contract specifically protects the rights of the homeowner to remain in their home for life or to rent it out and keep the rental income.

Through this model, Homesafe supports older homeowners to release wealth from their homes, without having to take on debt. Homesafe is not a reverse mortgage and continues to be the only debt freeway for seniors to access the wealth tied up in their homes, without interest or repayments of any kind. The Homesafe Wealth Release® solution is available to older Homeowners in Sydney and Melbourne subject to certain criteria.

Results – Value for Business and Society

Homesafe continues to receive an increasing number of enquiries and has assisted thousands of older homeowners, providing them with peace of mind in retirement by providing funding to help meet their living needs. Homesafe has generated positive social outcomes since 2005 by:

allowing older Australians the certainty of living in their homes for life, or until they choose to sell; and assisting thousands of 'asset rich, cash poor' homeowners to achieve a comfortable retirement by enabling access to the wealth tied up in their homes, debt-free. Funds have been used to pay down debt, conduct home maintenance, purchase cars and boats, fund travel etc. Homesafe has also generated strong

Exploring Shared Value

business outcomes The model has been highly successful for Homesafe and the joint venture partners. Along the way, Homesafe has created a portfolio that continues to grow. It is also generating a return to its shareholders consistent with investor expectations.

Since 2005 the portfolio has continued to grow. The table below shows the growth of the portfolio since June 2007. As of December 2017, the fair value of the portfolio was $709.8m.

Lessons Learned, Challenges and Outlook

Homesafe is a great example of a successfully shared value business model providing solid returns and great social outcomes. However, it has been a challenge to attract new funding partners. The Bendigo & Adelaide Bank is currently the sole funder of the Homesafe Trust. In order to continue to grow the product and potentially look for opportunities outside the current selected market, funding will be required from other partners. Further funding may assist in this product potentially becoming available to more senior homeowners in expanded geographical areas.

Given the uniqueness of this product, it has been a challenge in getting the investor market to understand the product and its contribution to the investor. Over the years there have been continuing discussions with potential funders to provide further information on how this product solves the funding needs for older Australians and the recognised contribution it makes both financially and socially.

Case Study 5: Supporting clients, colleagues and communities to rise

In 2018, Barclays was named on Fortune Magazine's 2018 "Change The World" list for the first time. The list was created to recognise companies that have had a positive social impact via activities that form part of their core business strategy.

Exploring Shared Value

For the past decade, employees at Barclays' offices around the world have been actively taking part in global and local initiatives that encourage the concept of shared value. Through its Social Innovation Facility (SIF), Barclays encourages colleagues to submit ideas that have commercial value whilst also solving pressing societal challenges. Many of these ideas have been funded and integrated into the business.

Globally Barclays is trying to address the employment gap both from the supply and the demand side. Through its Connect with Work programme, Barclays supports people into meaningful jobs and through the Unreasonable Impact, the programme supports growth-stage entrepreneurs to create thousands of jobs. This aligns well with Barclays' overall purpose of "creating opportunities to rise."

Barclays in the Asia Pacific

Exploring Shared Value

As part of its SIF activities, Barclays conducts an Intrapreneur Challenge. Employees across the Asia Pacific region are encouraged to submit ideas for a new product or service that could also have a positive impact on society. Selected colleagues win a place at the annual Intrapreneur Lab, held in Hong Kong in 2018, where employees attend workshops and receive coaching. The best ideas are then developed into a business plan and pitched to the senior leadership team for funding and approval to pilot.

"Barclays encourages and supports colleagues to participate in citizenship activities and programmes like these," says Anthony Davies, Chief Executive of Barclays Bank Plc Hong Kong Branch and Chair of Barclays' Asia Pacific Citizenship Council. "We want to give colleagues the opportunity to develop ideas that may extend beyond their day-to-day responsibilities."

Exploring Shared Value

Results and the way forward

Since 2012, approximately 50 social impact business ventures across the globe have been funded by Barclays' SIF. In some cases, employees have even created new internal opportunities for themselves. Overall, examples abound throughout the organisation of how Barclays is either initiating programmes for social change or teaming up with other organisations to benefit communities across the globe.

In 2018, Barclays established the Social Impact Banking group which identifies early-stage positive-impact companies and advises them on growing their businesses. Many industries provide opportunities for Barclays to provide support, such as sustainable agriculture, recycling, energy storage, electric transportation and financial services. A second focus of the group is building relationships with sustainability-focused investors across asset classes to better understand their needs and connect them with potential investments. The insight gained from both efforts will help Barclays advise larger corporates on trends and opportunities in these growing areas and how to engage with this new, differentiated investor base.

On an even larger scale, Barclays has partnered with the Unreasonable Group to launch the world's first international network of accelerators focused on scaling up entrepreneurial businesses that will help employ thousands worldwide, while solving some of our most pressing societal challenges. Unreasonable Impact consists of three intensive two-week programmes held annually in three distinct regions: the Americas, Asia Pacific, and the UK & Europe. In 2018, the Asia Pacific programme took place in June in Hong Kong and culminated in a"Demo Day" where 14 growth-stage ventures — fresh from consultations with an array of mentors and specialists from Barclays and other top firms — presented their ventures before a select group of invited guests. The global network consists of 90+

ventures that collectively reach approximately 105 million customers and support over 18,000 jobs in over 180 countries.

Shared Value and the Bottom Line

A series of tangible metrics from these initiatives enable the company to measure how the concepts are developing, from the idea stage to when they are launched. Internal "ambassadors" for the company help to spearhead continued progress within, while "Spotlight" sessions highlight programmes and initiatives that are emerging.

"They're fantastic, but I'd love to scale them up even more," says Davies of the programmes emerging at Barclays across the Asia-Pacific region. "Each year we're getting more people who are excited about it, so scalability is key…and that's about resources and funding."

Exploring Shared Value

The company is a firm believer that shared value programmes should be encouraged, no matter what the industry. "Things are changing so fast because of technology," adds Davies. "If you don't try and really think outside of the box and innovate, you're going to be left behind. Therefore, if you can embed that into your organisation and become innovative and creative, you've got a better chance of surviving. Barclays is investing the time, the money and the effort to educate employees about these initiatives. So it's good for us and it's good for the community."

Case Study 6: SHARED VALUE IN LIFE INSURANCE

Company Description

AIA Australia is an independent life insurance specialist with over 40 years of experience building successful partnerships. As a leading life insurer, AIA Australia offers a range of products that protect the financial health and welfare of more than three million Australians.

Exploring Shared Value

AIA Australia works closely with major financial institutions, superannuation funds and corporate partners. In addition, AIA Australia offers retail insurance products through financial advisers and a valued network of affinity partners.

AIA Australia is part of the AIA Group, a market leader in life insurance across the Asia Pacific region with almost 100 years' experience.

The Opportunity

Two in three Australians are currently overweight or obese and chronic disease is the leading cause of death and disability in the country. These preventive health challenges affect all sectors in Australia, including the life insurance industry. AIA Australia sees the impact of this first hand, with increasing numbers of life insurance claims made because of chronic diseases that affect a person's ability to work, causing financial strain and impacting on their quality of life and that of their families. Finding a way to halt this trend is critical for Australians to live better, longer and happier lives and to ensure a more sustainable future for our national health system.

The reach of AIA Australia's operations, and the role it plays in helping to protect over three million people, gives the company a unique position to create economic and social benefits for shareholders, customers, partners and society.

Traditionally, life insurers have limited engagement with policyholders until time of hardship and the need to make a claim. From the time of purchase until the point of making a claim, the main form of interaction with the life insurer is the renewal notice that comes in the post. With little engagement, many people lapse on their policies because they don't see the tangible value or reminder of being protected.

Lack of engagement with life insurance and the rising prevalence of the chronic disease, therefore, presents a unique opportunity for life insurers: How can a more tangible product be created that improves engagement with life insurance, the health of policyholders, and ultimately reduces the level and frequency of claims?

The Strategy

AIA Vitality In March 2014, AIA Australia launched Vitality, the world's leading health and wellness program, with more than 3.4 million members worldwide. Sold through independent financial advisers and key partners to people purchasing life insurance, the program uses the latest research in behavioural economics, incentivisation and wellness to stimulate people to take the first steps towards healthy living, and to make these lifestyle changes permanent. It is based on extensive research, which shows that consumers who make irrational health choices will generally take positive steps to improve their health if they are given a clear incentive to do so.

AIA Vitality members begin the program by completing health and fitness assessments and earn points for undertaking healthy activities, such as running and going to the gym. In addition, members are rewarded with points for displaying healthy behaviour, including discounts on shopping, entertainment and travel purchases and discounts on their insurance premiums.

Evidence for the efficacy of the program – in terms of improved clinical outcomes, reduced healthcare costs, lower hospital admissions, increased productivity at work and improved mortality rates – has been profiled in leading academic journals such as the American Journal of Health Promotion and the Harvard Business School1. While the program is just over two years old in Australia, it is expected to deliver similar results in terms of public health outcomes.

Exploring Shared Value

In the spirit of shared value, it is not just the policyholder/member that benefits from the Vitality program. By having a healthier pool of members that are less likely to claim in future and recover faster, AIA Australia can pass more savings back to them through higher discounted premiums and better rewards. Current data shows that policyholders that are heavily engaged on the program are up to 40 per cent less likely to lapse on their policy than those, not on AIA Vitality.

According to research compiled by AIA Australia and not-for-profit foundation Super Friend in 2013, if an employee is off work for 20 days, they have a 70 per cent chance of ever returning to work. If they are off for 45 days, this goes down to 50 per cent, and after 70 days their chance of ever returning to work is only 35 per cent. On a national scale, over 88 million days are lost to the Australian economy due to absenteeism, at a cost of $27.5 billion per annum in sick leave costs and lost productivity2. At the same time, the average duration for an income protection claim is 20 weeks (140 days). Reducing this average by just one week would save the insurance industry a total of $84 million a year.

By encouraging people to be healthier, both the incidence and duration of claims can be reduced, in turn reducing the direct costs to insurers and the broader costs to society. It is a win-win-win situation.

1 Porter, Michael E., Kramer, Mark R., and Aldo Sesia. "Discovery Limited." Harvard Business School Case 715-423, December 2014. (Revised May 2015.)

2 Medibank & PwC Workplace Wellness in Australia 2010

Exploring Shared Value

Results – Value for Business and Society

Overview of the outcomes of implementing the shared value strategy.

Social outcomes:

- Healthier Vitality members
- Rewarded behaviour for proactive members
- Improved mortality rates
- Shared data to improve wellness Business outcomes:
- Improved clinical outcomes
- Lower hospital admissions
- Increased productivity in the workplace
- Reduced claim periods
- Reduced premiums

Lessons Learned, Challenges and Outlook

For AIA Australia, the AIA Vitality program shows how shared value is working in the life insurance industry. AIA Vitality seeks to intervene in claims before they hit the door of the life insurer for preventable chronic diseases while providing a program to improve the health of members and the wider public. It's about making life insurance tangible and engaging daily. This program is just the beginning of AIA Australia's shared value journey.

Case Study 7: Smart Power for Rural Development, Creating a Sustainable Market Solution to Energy Poverty

Rohit Chandra is passionate about powering rural economies with electricity— specifically, bringing power to the more than 300 million rural Indians who currently lack it. Without rural electricity, the most remote and economically at-risk populations in India also lack the means to grow their businesses, educate their children, and access health services. "For me, this is much more than a job," Chandra says. "We see the potential to have a huge social impact by using a more grassroots power model that can profitably serve the base of the pyramid consumer market." 1

Exploring Shared Value

To follow through on this passion, Chandra cofounded OMC Power, a renewable energy services company (ESCO) based on the idea that demand will increase if electricity is made affordable and reliable in rural areas. (2)

2 OMC is the pioneer of a unique and innovative "ABC" model, whereby it provides power to telecom towers as "A"anchor loads, rural small and medium "B"usiness enterprises, and rural "C"ommunities via reliable solar mini-grid power plants that produce approximately 25-100 kilowatts (kW). Chandra's dream is to facilitate the economic empowerment of rural Indians by growing OMC into the world's largest rural electrification company. (3)

OMC is committed to build 1,000 solar mini-grid power plants in the next four to five years and scale to 25,000 in the next 10 years, capturing at least 20% of the Indian mini-grid market. (4)

He also sees great opportunity for innovation. His goal is to reduce the cost of electricity production by half within the next three years. (5)

Exploring Shared Value

As OMC reduces these costs, Chandra says, "we will soon be at an inflexion point—the market will explode and we will be the innovators and the first movers."(6)

Chandra has 30-plus years of experience in the telecom space, and his experience has convinced him that the rural electricity sector, like mobile telecommunications, lends itself to extraordinary economies of scale if the business model is implemented successfully. (7)

By delivering electricity to rural businesses, which can increase output and productivity with a reliable source of power, OMC is significantly improving local economies. As one OMC customer who was accustomed to spotty electricity from unreliable generators noted, "When electricity came, it was like magic... [A] 24/7 power supply raised my earnings by around Rs 40,000 [~USD $600] a month. Most of the irrigation pumps in the area operate only for a few hours a day because there is no electricity. But I can run [my pump] up to 16 hours a day."(8)

Exploring Shared Value

Providing cost-effective and reliable electricity has the potential to dramatically improve long-term prosperity and well-being in the developing world, building a more resilient and inclusive rural economy.

Introduction

The Rockefeller Foundation is supporting ESCOs* such as OMC, DESI Power,

Tara Urja, and others to create shared value through its Smart Power for Rural

Development Initiative. Shared value is a management approach that enables companies to increase profits, reduce costs, and enhance competitiveness by solving social problems, such as limited access to electricity. Rockefeller's Smart Power for Rural Development Initiative provides affordable financing to ESCOs and links them to an ecosystem of Rockefeller grant-funded partners, which provide project and business development support as well as policy and regulatory recommendations.

Exploring Shared Value

Rockefeller's partners are coordinated by Smart Power India, a Rockefeller-incubated entity and wholly-owned subsidiary. The Foundation set an ambitious target to reach one thousand villages within the first three years of the initiative, with a goal of building a viable market quickly and spurring interest, action, and innovation among key players in the ecosystem.

Rockefeller's strategy to support the shared value ecosystem for renewable

mini-grids is already delivering significant results for ESCOs. OMC is seeing

a rise in its number of rural business customers and enhanced community

engagement—and, as a result, higher revenue. (9)

Beyond direct business results, OMC is experiencing considerably enhanced brand recognition—critical for a market still unfamiliar to investors. (10)

Exploring Shared Value

As Chandra notes, "Rockefeller plays a very important role in providing the needed financing and visibility for the sector in general, reducing overall market risk and making other lenders more comfortable in investing."(11)

The Problem and the Opportunity Despite great effort and the huge sums of money spent on promoting the expansion of national grids, poor rural communities worldwide continue to lack affordable and reliable electricity. For 1.3 billion people (18% of the global population), accessing electricity to power homes and businesses remains a distant reality. (12)

95% of the 1.3 billion live in either Sub-Saharan Africa or developing Asia, and 84% live in rural areas. (13)

304 million, or nearly one in four, live in India—making it home to the largest un-electrified population in the world. (14)

Exploring Shared Value

In India, only 67% of households in rural areas have access to electricity, compared to 94% in urban areas. (15)

In some predominantly rural states, such as Bihar and Uttar Pradesh, only 10% of the population has access to electricity. (16)

The Indian national government recognizes the lack of access to electricity as a social concern, and there are programs in place to extend grids in rural areas where access to electricity is the lowest. (17)

However, according to an industry report, "progress has been slow, and the number of underserved households is e9xpected to decline by only 5% over the next 10 years."(18)

Lack of access to reliable electricity has a negative impact on social and economic development, limiting people's ability to enhance their incomes, improve their health, increase their food security, educate their children, and access key information services.

(19) It especially burdens women with physically taxing activities and decreased safety. (20) Lack of access to electricity constraints rural business development by increasing operational costs and lowering agricultural productivity. (21) Perhaps most importantly, it is a major barrier to achieving a more inclusive economy and to building the resilience of poor or vulnerable populations.

In India, at least half of rural household power demand will need to be met by solutions beyond the traditional grid. (22) While a range of rural electrification solutions such as solar lanterns and solar home

systems are available for basic household lighting, few meet the needs of multiple productive electricity users, including rural infrastructure (e.g., telecom towers, banking facilities, gas stations), rural businesses (e.g., milk chillers, agro-mills, cold-storage), and rural households. Mini-grids provide a unique solution because of their ability to connect rural businesses and industries to reliable and affordable power—spurring local economic development. As Jaideep Mukherji, CEO of Smart Power India, noted, "I worked with solar lanterns for some years, but kept getting the question:

'What's next? We want to work and have an income. We need more energy.' [The rural poor] desire to have the same electrical connection as anyone else, [and] solar devices would never meet these needs.

It's about powering economic activity."(23) There is growing interest among businesses, the government, and policymakers to address energy poverty. Renewable mini-grids are increasingly being recognized as a key solution to address the inability of the national grid to meet those most in need. Increased penetration of telecom towers in rural areas with high demand for affordable and reliable electricity and the growth of rural economies are creating 1.3 billion people globally lack access to electricity

Exploring Shared Value

THE PROBLEM THE OPPORTUNITY

It will take 20-25 years for the least electrified states to be fully grid-connected

1. Ministry of Power, Rockefeller team analysis Nearly 1 in 4 without

access to electricity live in India A catalyzed rural electricity market that accelerates inclusive economic growth, community resilience, and provides other positive outcomes for the poor and vulnerable Renewable ESCOs can

provide affordable, reliable and clean electricity Telecom towers, rural

businesses and households need affordable, reliable electricity sustainable demand sources for ESCOs. Other rural anchor loads, such as irrigation pumps, can also provide significant demand. One report estimates that the total market size for decentralized renewable energy systems in India could be $150 million by 2018.24 Rockefeller identified the importance of large institutional or anchor customers as an important first step in helping ESCOs take advantage of the market opportunity. Serving only businesses and households can be difficult due to spikes in demand or insufficient demand to spread costs out over a wider group. Anchor loads, which consume more consistently and reliably and are therefore able to sign long-term power purchase agreements, help improve the financial sustainability of the ESCO model. Rockefeller explored which anchor customers could play this role. In India, telecom towers were a natural candidate because of their deep penetration in rural markets, increasing energy demand, and high operating costs due to the use of expensive diesel fuel.

The Indian telecom tower industry provides potential opportunities for ESCOs to realize economies of scale. A single telecom company can directly or indirectly own 100,000 of the country's 400,000 total towers. (25), 26 India's growing demand for mobile phones—from 6.4 million subscribers in 2002 to 752 million subscribers in 2010—has driven the proliferation of towers. (27) Energy demand from these telecom towers is projected to grow 13% per year, with less than half supplied via the grid. (28) Most telecom towers in rural locations use expensive diesel fuel,(29) resulting in higher operating costs and reduced profitability.

The revenue potential for electricity providers serving rural telecom towers alone in India is forecasted to grow to at least $95 million by 2018,30 which should increase with a recent government mandate that 50% of all rural telecom towers shift to renewable energy. (31)

Those ESCOs that have been providing solar power to telecom towers are now considering expanding their consumer bases to include households and rural enterprises.32 Smaller ESCOs, which have traditionally served rural households, are interested in supplying electricity to telecom towers or other rural anchors, such as irrigation pumps, as well as to local businesses. By electrifying telecom towers, rural businesses, and households, the mini-grid delivery model strengthens the financial viability of ESCOs, improves the productivity of rural businesses, and increases access to lighting for households— contributing to overall economic opportunity and a more inclusive economy. A more dynamic rural economy, in turn, leads to an increase in the consumer base of paying electricity consumers.

Business Needs and Barriers to Scale

Beginning in 2010, Rockefeller undertook a period of research, analysis, prototyping, and testing to better understand the ecosystem of organizations involved in rural electrification and the barriers to scaling potential solutions. Rockefeller established a set of pilot mini-grid plants to begin to test project development tools; link ESCOs to NGOs to foster improved community engagement; explore opportunities for standardization, innovation, and bulk purchasing to reduce technology costs; build financial models to identify risk capital needs, and identify policies and regulations that would strengthen

market confidence. (33) Rockefeller's leadership on the research and design phase demonstrates the unique role that foundations, as neutral entities with the ability to de-risk new markets in unfamiliar geographies, can play in helping a broad range of stakeholders understand past system failures and

identify the key leverage points for change. In the Indian market, ESCOs struggle to reach scale due to concerns over demand, operational constraints related to doing business in rural areas, uncertainty over the policy and regulatory environment, and lack of access to financial capital. This represents the classic pioneer gap, where a market-based solution

has the potential to drive change at scale, but requires external support, such as philanthropic funding, to be fully realized. (34) Each of the following business needs formed the building blocks for Rockefeller's Smart Power for Rural Development approach.

ESCOs need assuring, predictable demand: Rockefeller found that facilitating power purchase agreements (PPAs) between ESCOs and telecom tower operators would provide a baseline level of demand, enabling ESCOs to more quickly recover upfront plant construction costs and sell electricity

to rural businesses and households. Pooja Raman, Legal Counsel and Investment Lead for OMC Power says, "Apart from telecom towers, we focus on rural business because they assure the needed electricity demand to make the project feasible."(35) Desi Power, an ESCO focused on clean, affordable power provision in rural India, connects with smaller local industry to aggregate demand and calibrate supply. However, though renewable electricity is often cheaper than kerosene and diesel, rural consumers are sceptical. (36)

Exploring Shared Value

Consumers wait to ensure alternatives to established energy sources are reliable.37 Businesses are often seasonal, making it difficult to properly size a grid and balance load. Also, ESCOs lack data on rural consumers' needs and willingness to pay. This leads to an unpredictable load ramp-up timeline, reducing ESCOs' ability to plan and allocate resources. Ensuring sustained demand remains a key barrier to scale for ESCOs.

ESCOs require the skills and experience to serve rural markets and reduce technology costs: Many ESCOs have been traditionally focused on selling to telecom towers or to consumers and businesses in high-density urban areas. Therefore, they lack experience and the skills necessary to create and maintain a rural customer base, and perceive risk around collecting payments, and often lack the knowledge to successfully site a plant that will serve multiple electricity customers (e.g., households, rural businesses, anchor loads, etc.).(38) In addition, fragmented supply chains and low order volumes create high technology sourcing costs for solar panels, batteries, and mini-grid components, further limiting the scalability of the model.

ESCOs need access to low-cost capital and government subsidies: Since the business model delivers modest financial returns, involves high risk, and requires a long-term investment, ESCOs struggle to access low-cost capital. The financial viability of the business model is heavily dependent upon the cost and availability of the funds required for the initial capital investment, the speed with which consumers are connected to the power source and their payments collected, and the availability and timeliness of funding from government subsidies from the Ministry of New and Renewable Energy (MNRE). (39)

For example, the internal rate of return (IRR) on a mini-grid project is reduced by nearly half when the ESCO does not receive a government subsidy from the MNRE.(40)

ESCOs need a regulatory environment that reduces risk and is conducive to the long-term growth of the market: The lack of clarity around the Indian government's grid extension plans and difficulty in accessing government subsidy has led to some scepticism about the viability of the ESCO business

model. Raman notes, "The biggest challenge that we face right now is that this industry is relatively unregulated, so we don't have a clear-cut policy around mini-grids, thus no framework within which we need to operate."(41) In addition, the uncertainty around the long-term strategy for linkages between the mini-grid and the main grid—whether the mini-grid will become the last-mile distributor or feed into the main grid directly—makes it challenging to obtain visibility into the long-term model.

The developmental phase of the initiative, which included ground-level prototyping, also focused on developing an understanding of the needs and aspirations of rural customers and creating a business model to address those needs affordably. Through this intentional process and the active development of the above hypotheses in collaboration with private sector actors, Rockefeller was in a strong position to develop the market-based platform and suite of services needed to catalyze action in the sector.

As Sanjay Khazanchi, an independent consultant and implementing partner since the beginning of the initiative in 2010, remarked, "This phase was really about laying the groundwork for the program. We established a very strong platform in which to engage all of the various stakeholders. The market-based approach makes the model a bit challenging, but at the same time sustainable."(42)

The Rockefeller Foundation's Approach: Fostering Shared Value Ecosystems for Rural Power

In 2014, the Foundation officially launched the Smart Power for Rural Development initiative by committing $75 million (including $10 million in the exploratory phase) in grant funding and affordable loans† to an ecosystem of partners, including ESCOs, NGOs, and civil society organizations. With a goal of demonstrating the financial viability of the market, it set the ambitious target of connecting one thousand villages and one million people to renewable mini-grid plants. Connecting one thousand villages provides the scale necessary to bring credibility to the business model and demonstrate the investment opportunity for the private sector.

To quickly demonstrate results, encourage new partnerships, and build the evidence base of what works, Rockefeller fast-tracked 26 plants during the summer of 2014. These plants provided an important platform to test and validate various assumptions about the business model and to build momentum in the market. According to Clare Boland Ross, Associate Director of the Rockefeller Foundation, "The main plan was to get some plants on the ground so we could start validating and challenging assumptions in the model. This was important to act as a proof point for both telecoms and ESCOs. It has turned out to be even more valuable than we thought, as we learned so much through the implementation and can now continue to use these sites as a way to test and showcase new innovations before rolling them out to ESCOs."(43)

Smart Power's vision is to accelerate inclusive economic growth, community resilience, and other positive outcomes (e.g., improved access to education, increased health and safety, improved women's empowerment, etc.) for poor and vulnerable people in India by catalyzing a rural energy transformation. The approach centres on a simple but profound realization: in order to catalyse the market for renewable mini-grids that serve multiple users, the Foundation must work in close collaboration with partners to demonstrate a financially viable business model and address barriers to scale.

Addressing barriers to scale

The Foundation fosters the creation of a shared value partnership ecosystem that strengthens the financial viability of ESCOs by focusing on three critical components of rural electricity delivery: electricity supply, electricity demand, and the enabling environment. To coordinate these various partners, Rockefeller established Smart Power India to be a strategic advisor to the ESCO market, providing financing, project, and business development support.

On the electricity demand side, Smart Power India partners such as Technology and Action for Rural Advancement (TARA) help ESCOs develop demand generation strategies to convert rural businesses to renewables, enable new rural businesses to start-up and expand, and educate consumers about the benefits of renewable energy. Partners such as PANI help with community engagement and general marketing and visibility.

On the electricity supply side, Smart Power India and its partners, including CKinetics, help to promote adoption of best practices and subsidize initial start-up costs by (i) providing project development support (e.g., site selection, energy assessment, project feasibility reports); (ii) sharing on-the-ground learnings and emergent innovations across a network of ESCOs (e.g., collection methodologies, metering);

(iii) providing training on practical business development tools (e.g., models for plant economics, data collection tools, standardized contracts with customers and suppliers); and (iv) facilitating bulk procurement and investment in technology innovation to reduce costs. (44)

Within the enabling environment, Smart Power India works to bring greater clarity to the policy and regulatory environment and increase access to financing options. Rockefeller's main policy partner, Shakti Sustainable Energy Foundation, helps inform policies and regulations in India that impact the

growth of the mini-grid market. Shakti is currently working with the MNRE, the Central Electric Regulation Commission, and the various state regulatory commissions to develop state and national mini-grid policy frameworks to answer three key questions:(45)

• Where and when will the national grid most likely be extended, and what geographies should be prioritized by off-grid solutions?

• What government financial and non-financial support will be available for mini-grids?

• What will be the protocol for connecting mini-grids to the traditional grid?

Shakti works closely with other Rockefeller Foundation partners, including ESCOs and NGOs, to incorporate a diverse range of opinions into the policy framework development process. As Deepak Gupta, Senior Program Manager (Power) at Shakti, noted, "These multiple perspectives help us define our policy prescriptions. We don't want to lose out on any good ideas. We reach out to each partner one-on-one and the group to get their perspectives, host debates, and try to help engender cross-pollination of ideas around the policy." (46)

To get ESCO businesses off the ground, Rockefeller provides financing through program-related investments (PRIs). A pioneer, the Foundation has been making PRIs—investments expected to generate both social impact and a concessionary financial return—since the 1990s. In the case of Smart Power India, Rockefeller is investing approximately $23 million in PRIs. The use of proceeds for the PRIs is to partially finance the capital expenditures incurred by the ESCOs when building plants. ESCOs are required

to raise debt and equity to finance the remainder of the cost of the plants. To ensure social impact, the Rockefeller loan agreements require ESCOs to provide a substantial proportion of their electricity to rural businesses and households. In addition, Rockefeller's support reduces the risk for other potential impact investors and funders to enter the market, and increased financial viability of ESCOs serves to reinforce the investor value proposition.

Providing a range of services

Today, Smart Power India contracts with existing Rockefeller Foundation-funded grantees but will eventually move toward a more autonomous selection process, directly contracting with support partners. Ultimately, the goal is for Smart Power India to attract additional investment as well as potentially its own revenue streams so that it can directly offer services to ESCOs. In the end, of course, the ultimate objective is to create a self-sustaining market for renewable ESCOs.

As Jaideep Mukherji notes, "I think it would be SPI's ambition to put itself out of business. If we can create a self-propagating and commercially sustainable system with private capital coming in and a supportive government, that would be a tremendous success for SPI and a legacy that the

Exploring Shared Value

Rockefeller Foundation would be really proud of."47 Smart Power's partners provide services across this ecosystem to address the business needs and barriers to scale that inhibit the overall growth of the ESCO market.

Exploring Shared Value

FIGURE 2 SMART POWER INDIA SERVICES TO ADDRESS ESCO BUSINESS NEEDS

ENABLING ENVIRONMENT	ELECTRICITY SUPPLY	ELECTRICITY DEMAND
Policy/Regulatory	Renewable Mini Grid Energy Services Company (ESCO)	Rural Households
Funders/Financiers		Rural Businesses
	Project, business, and technology development support providers	Anchor Loads

FIGURE 3 SMART POWER INDIA PARTNERSHIP ECOSYSTEM

Figure 2 illustrates these business needs and the range of services that Smart Power India provides, and Figure 3 showcases the initiative's partnership ecosystem. These elements showcase the comprehensive approach the Foundation has taken to support the growth of shared value solutions in this marketplace.

Exploring Shared Value

OMC POWER SHARED VALUE PARTNERSHIP

Engaging with communities and rural businesses to build a strong presence in rural markets requires OMC, an ESCO based in New Delhi, to build new capabilities to generate the needed demand. The company faces challenges in acquiring rural customers, developing the business model for new markets, getting the needed approvals for project development, and complying with local and state regulations. OMC's partnership with the Rockefeller Foundation and Smart Power India enables OMC to quickly deepen relationships with rural businesses and local communities in order to connect rural consumers in a cost-efficient manner. Smart Power India provides value to OMC in three distinct ways, resulting in direct business benefits:

1. Customer acquisition: Smart Power India partners help connect OMC to potential rural businesses, enabling the company to acquire

rural customers and increase revenue and reduce costs.

2. Business modelling: Rockefeller-provided data analytics on the size and composition of the potential electricity consumers in each village help OMC properly size its plants to meet demand and load ramp-up needs, resulting

in higher profitability and reduced costs.

3. • Policy advocacy, influence and visibility: Smart Power India brings greater clarity to the mini-grid development and financing process— critical to increasing investor confidence, reducing risk, and strengthening long-term

Policy advocacy, influence and visibility: Smart Power India brings greater clarity to the mini-grid development and financing process—critical to increasing investor confidence, reducing risk, and strengthening long-term

access to affordable capital. Due in part to the partnership with Rockefeller, OMC is poised for future growth and expansion in the Indian mini-grid market. OMC has leveraged Rockefeller's brand reputation and ecosystem of partnerships to raise the visibility of its business model and importantly enter into discussions with domestic and foreign capital providers. According

to Chandra, "I think that many pieces of this are continually evolving towards positive outcomes; the business model is getting more and more refined, streamlining expenditures across units. We are driving it, lots of players

are driving it. Cost of production could be reduced by half in the next three years. Rockefeller will continue to play a key role in helping to scale the model."

DESI POWER SHARED VALUE PARTNERSHIP

DESI Power's leadership has long believed that traditional electricity grid extension efforts will not be able to meet the development needs of India's villages that lack access to reliable power. In 1996, the company began to

Exploring Shared Value

develop an integrated electricity solution for India's rural poor. As DESI Power

founder Dr Hari Sharan notes, "We have to look at these three aspects—social, environmental, and economic value—simultaneously. Any business has to be profitable, but we do not try to maximize profit at the expense of the village development—we actively work with villages to generate the demand via small businesses that also have a social impact. Electricity is used as the motor of development rather than the end in and of itself." To measure impact, the company has developed a robust monitoring system that tracks various social metrics, including job creation and agricultural productivity.

This social impact ethos parlays into DESI's primary focus on developing local economies through electricity delivery.

Rather than taking a telecom tower-focused approach, DESI connects smaller-scale but growing industrial actors—such as irrigation pump operators, water companies, energy service businesses, and cold storage companies—to the mini-grid system. Effectively matching electricity supply to the various needs of different types of consumers and enterprises, with daily and seasonal load variation, is the key to the profitability of the business model. DESI

works closely with Smart Power India partners that provide financing and training to electricity providers and rural businesses.

DESI has benefited substantially from a partnership with Rockefeller:

1. Building load demand: Smart Power India has connected DESI to enterprise development providers and improved the company's internal capacity to effectively target rural enterprises from project management, plant

construction, and O&M and training through scale.

2. Financing rural businesses: Smart Power India has identified other sources of financing for rural businesses, facilitating stronger local economies and generating more demand.

3. Improving visibility: Smart Power India's integrated approach is beginning to demonstrate the viability of the model to potential investors and policymakers. Dr Hari Sharan envisions a future in which all 700 villages in Araria district will have their own power plants and enterprises, starting with 100 power stations in 100 villages within the next three to four years. Over the longer term, he hopes the system will evolve so that a national power system consisting of centralized and decentralized grids sources 40-60% of its power from CO_2-emission-free mini-grids. These partnerships will ultimately lead to a

sustainable business model that secures greater access to electricity and jobs for India's rural poor.

Results to Date

Exploring Shared Value

The Rockefeller Foundation and Smart Power India teams have embedded learning and evaluation throughout their approach. The Foundation leverages a subset of mini-grid plants to continually prototype

and test business model innovations before offering them to the ESCO network. Smart Power India has also implemented a systematic monitoring and evaluation process that informs strategic decision making and enables adaptive management of its projects. Operating at three levels, the monitoring and evaluation process involves 1) close-to-real time information on the implementation of power plants through the Smart Power Implementation Monitoring System (SIMS); 2) monitoring of intermediate and

longer-term outcomes; and 3) independent impact evaluation and rapid reviews of key socioeconomic metrics such as income generation, education, and health improvements.

Exploring Shared Value

SIMS analytics have been used by grantees, ESCOs, and the Foundation to identify risks in implementation and support ongoing learning efforts, around ensuring Smart Power India's services are meet

ESCO business needs.48 The independent impact evaluations highlight gaps in addressing customers' concerns and offer recommendations for ways that ESCOs can improve their processes to increase customers' satisfaction.

Since the launch of the full initiative in mid-2014, Rockefeller has focused on improving the economics of the business model, sharing insights among a diverse network of partners, and transitioning key roles and responsibilities to the Smart Power India entity.49 As of January 2016, the Rockefeller Foundation has facilitated the development of 85 renewable mini-grid plants.50 These plants are currently supplying quality power to more than 15,000 people, 1,952 rural businesses, and 81 telecom towers.51 A first step to

achieve the initiative's objective to reach one thousand villages is to motivate rural consumers to switch to renewable energy—and use it to develop and expand local businesses, enhancing the local economy.

ESCOs are responding to evidence of increasingly sustainable rural electricity demand. Increased demand for power from households and businesses

• Shift from diesel power to renewable power: In the most recent data from July 2014, seven in ten households and eight in ten rural businesses are using the power from the mini-grid as their primary source of electricity. For rural business consumers using Smart Power mini-grids, diesel generator use has been reduced by 84%, and kerosene lamp use has been reduced by 90%.52 For household consumers using Smart Power mini-grids, kerosene lamp use has been reduced by 72%. This shift from diesel and kerosene lamps to renewable power indicates that consumers perceive significant

benefits from renewable power. The main reasons consumers are willing to switch to renewable energy include enhanced reliability and consistency of supply, increased supply hours, improved quality of light, and reduced costs.

• Increasing demand for renewable electricity: After experiencing consistent and reliable Smart Power connections, many consumers indicate a willingness to consume more power (some diversify consumption by adding more appliances, including fans and televisions) and also pay proportionately more for it. This has built confidence among rural businesses, leading to observed increased operating hours. For rural business consumers using Smart Power mini-grids, electricity demand has increased

by 33%. For household consumers using Smart Power mini-grids, electricity demand has increased by 25%. Anecdotal evidence points to telecoms reducing operating costs through shifting from diesel

to solar power.

Socio-economic impacts

• The improved overall vibrancy of the local economy:

Evidence from Smart Power-connected consumers points to increased hours of operation for rural businesses and village markets, suggesting a more

vibrant local economy. Smart Power is connecting businesses that have a wide range of social and economic benefits including pharmacies and

learning support centres (for school tutoring and computer instruction).

• Education: Smart Power-connected households are using added hours of electricity for studying, leading to qualitative evidence that indicates children are more engaged in school. Parents also suggest that brighter Smart Power LED bulbs make studying more comfortable and less stressful for their children's eyes.

• Health: Households perceive reduced eye problems due to elimination of flickering lights.53

• Enhanced sense of safety: Smart Power consumers perceive greater safety, particularly among women and young girls, due to more reliable street lights.

• Improved quality of life: Women suggest that availability of consistent and luminescent light makes their engagement in household chores more convenient. With a reliable and predictable supply, they have more time available for socializing and leisure activities.

Business Impacts (ESCOs, and rural businesses)

It is still too early in the project's implementation process to fully demonstrate business outcomes. However, below are some early results for ESCOs and rural businesses:

Exploring Shared Value

ESCOS

• By the end of the first quarter of 2016, 100 plants are up and running with plans to bring more online, demonstrating ongoing interest from the market

• Bulk purchasing of parts resulted in discounts of 6-7% for the first 30 ESCOs working with the initiative

• Performance has varied widely across sites with some performing well and others lagging behind targets. Local teams are studying these differences to identify the conditions and interventions that drive success

• The model is well-known among sector stakeholders and has generated a strong appetite to learn more and engage with the initiative going forward

Exploring Shared Value

RURAL BUSINESSES

• Significant ground-work has been done to create new rural businesses

• About three-quarters of rural businesses reported an expanded customer base

• When connected, rural businesses save significant money on monthly energy expenditures, resulting in increased income and business expansion(54)

Lessons Learned

Despite the achievements listed in the previous section, Rockefeller is facing challenges related to meeting the scale (number of plants) and efficiency targets of the ESCOs (revenue and cost targets) that were originally outlined. These challenges are not surprising given the nascent nature of the market.

Three lessons that potentially shed light on these challenges include:(55)

Exploring Shared Value

1. Actual costs are higher and revenue is harder to capture than originally anticipated. Given the early stage of the market, it is unsurprising that a focus on improving plant-level economies will be important. The Foundation is beginning to address this by investing in innovations to help bring

down the cost of capital expenses and by supporting the growth of rural businesses.

2. More flexibility is required to meet the needs of the market. A private sector-led approach to the energy market requires less prescriptive approaches to outcomes and solutions. This will require Rockefeller to continue to evolve the model to allow for the unique needs of each ESCO, and facilitate innovative responses and strategies to market pressures and individual customer needs.

3. ESCOs value financing support and diversified services, but different business models will

continue to require tailored offerings. Individual ESCOs have different business considerations, existing skills, and unique gaps in their capabilities. The Rockefeller Foundation has realized that this diverse pool of partners has needs that cannot be met with a "one-size-fits-all" support package. As the model evolves, a focus remains on customization of services to the specific strengths, challenges, and needs of each ESCO.

These insights have enabled the Rockefeller Foundation to build greater flexibility into the business model by broadening engagement to new potential institutional/anchor load customers, identifying areas of innovation to bring down costs, more effectively tailoring services to different types of ESCOs, and focusing efforts on local economic development to ensure continuous growth in the demand for power. More detail on each of these insights is offered below.

Exploring Shared Value

1. Creating a flexible business model with the potential to engage additional anchor industries:

The opportunity for telecom towers is clear—they are located in many rural villages without access to electricity and ensure a steady demand base. However, Rockefeller has learned that the key is to develop a diverse and healthy load mix, and that telecom towers are only part of the solution.

Servicing a telecom tower comes with its own challenges, requiring the ESCO to provide continuous, uninterrupted power for 99.9% of the time. ESCOs are penalized financially by tower owners for every minute of downtime.

Therefore, Smart Power India seeks to engage additional anchor industries including financial institutions/ATMs, water irrigation systems, and fuel stations, among others. By creating a healthy mix of different customers, Smart Power India strives to ensure that ESCOs are not overly reliant on one or two anchor loads to provide reliable demand. As Smart Power India CEO Mukherji notes, "We always wanted to create some flexibility in the business model. It is not just telecom towers that can be the anchor loads

and provide the demand that ESCOs need. If these entities help us achieve the impact we want to achieve, we should embrace them."56

Driving new business model innovations to bring down the cost of electricity distribution and promote more efficient use: In its first year of operation, Smart Power identified payment collection inefficiency, load ramp-up, and technology costs as significant drivers of higher CAPEX and OPEX

costs. To address these concerns, Rockefeller is currently in the process of standardizing a variety of technical and operational tools to improve the profitability of the business model. For example, the Foundation put more energy into bulk purchasing contracts for technology parts and identified mechanisms needed to incentivize connecting productive loads. Another prospective strategy would be to engage partners to implement mobile payment collection and pre-paid metering.

3. Tailoring services to a broad range of ESCOs: Each ESCO is unique in its strengths and capabilities. Some are already well connected to the community and do not need Smart Power's support to engage

consumers. Others need assistance with technical issues, business processes, or partnerships with telecoms. Smart Power India must, therefore, build each ESCO relationship based on its strengths and weaknesses. As Khazanchi notes, "After we worked with many ESCOs to build more

plants, we realized that it is absolutely critical to customize ESCO services based off of their specific business needs."57

4. Keeping rural business as a central focus: Mini-grid connections alone don't automatically make rural businesses successful. The Rockefeller Foundation understood the need for a much more concerted effort to develop rural businesses that meet local needs and have access to a market to

supply their goods and services. The Foundation views the focus on rural business development as central to achieving the economic growth that it seeks. To this end, it is working with grassroots development agencies which are specialized in providing services to build the capacities of rural

business. Rockefeller is also cultivating other corporate partners who are planning to extend their supply chain into villages where ESCO mini-grids are located. Rockefeller has created a village level Gross Domestic Product (GDP) tool to track changes of GDP within the Smart Power mini-grid

coverage area. This data will help Rockefeller understand overall market dynamics in order to provide the necessary services to scale rural businesses.

Looking Ahead

The Rockefeller Foundation understands that the rural electrification challenge is complex, and that technological intervention will not be sufficient in moving the needle and achieving long-lasting change

for rural economies. With hundreds of millions of Indians still without access to reliable electricity, the need for a financially viable, market-driven, and the systemic solution is urgent. The Foundation critically framed the problem not just as electricity access for access's sake, but through the prism of market

development and serving the electricity needs of a growing rural economy—ensuring that renewable mini-grid ESCOs are linked to demand from rural businesses and households.

To date, Smart Power India has progressed toward providing a sustainable solution to the

Exploring Shared Value

local energy crisis. The initiative has developed a business model and is actively addressing barriers to scale. Through this work, the Foundation has fostered the creation of a shared value partnership ecosystem, leveraging its influence and convening power to bridge key stakeholder divides and develop a sustainable solution

that provided mutually beneficial solutions for households, rural businesses, telecoms, ESCOs, and the broader system. Smart Power India, in collaboration with its partners, has brought significant experience

and expertise to the renewable mini-grid market, helping to develop the initiative into a market leader and one-stop-shop where ESCOs can access financing, refine a viable business model, and identify consumer engagement strategies. An iterative process, the Foundation is committed to improving energy access in India and beyond and expects to continuously refine the business model and its own interventions to most effectively address the barrier to scale.

Exploring Shared Value

As Rockefeller seeks to achieve its goal of providing renewable electricity to one thousand villages in India—a target selected for its significant need, market opportunity, and potential to demonstrate scalability—it is also developing the business case to utilize the same principles globally while taking local factors into account. To do so, it will continue to prove the business model in India, position Smart Power India as the market facilitator, and begin to understand the key contextual factors of other rural areas

in India, Southeast Asia, and Africa. These new markets will likely have vastly different considerations, needs, and solutions, but the Smart Power India model can provide a set of principles and key insights that will drive adoption and impact within different contexts.

The greatest opportunities (and challenges) for the Rockefeller Foundation and the Smart Power model in its next phase include:

Exploring Shared Value

• Improving plant-level economics: Anchor loads remain critical for stronger economics, and the definition has widened to incorporate "tenants" beyond telecom towers to bring down costs. The Foundation is also working with technology partners to invest in innovations that will bring down

the cost of mini-grids thereby improving plant-level economics. Additionally, the Foundation has determined that increasing ramp-up speed by providing access to affordable consumer goods such as energy-efficient fans and televisions will help meet customer needs, increase demand, and improve

service delivery. Rockefeller will continue to identify tools and processes that can help strengthen the business model across these many dimensions.

• Making a strong case for public and private sector engagement: Continued investment in a replicable learning agenda and strong messaging on key successes will enhance advocacy efforts and build support among policymakers. In addition, these proof points will also strengthen private

sector engagement and promote market-driven investment and innovation.

• Expanding and replicating the model: With the proof point being developed in India, Rockefeller is starting to look at other countries that would be well-positioned to support decentralized power. The model will need to be adapted to meet the social and business needs of future replication sites and their contexts and enabling environments.

The Smart Power model has tremendous opportunity for replication across markets, and potential for enabling economic development in rural communities at scale. The Rockefeller Foundation's unique ecosystems approach to market-based solutions in this sector showcases the benefits of complex partnerships for shared value and the value-add that de-risking investments by innovative investors can play in

Exploring Shared Value

creating new opportunities for both business and society to flourish.

Chapter 3

Review of Case Studies

This chapter would enable us to review the 7 case studies drawn from different sectors, clearly stated in chapter 2 and we can see the win-win situation concept, reasons why Africa should be in the forefront with respect to embracing this ideology.

Case study 1 describes the fading Cha chaan tengs tea culture in hong kong , Friesland Campina Hong Kong saw an opportunity with this societal issue and decided to resolve it by providing training for the unemployed youths, the training was formal by the involvement of Restaurants whose function was to draw up the curriculum. The training program was very effective, this led to the production of entrepreneurs with relevant skills, though the percentage is very insignificant compared to the unemployed population, the effort should be recognised.

The culture was preserved because cafés sprang up, where the local milk tea is prepared and sold to the public. This revived the dying culture and on the other hand FCMK's product 'Black&White' evaporated milk is one of the component of the local milk tea, 10,000 cups of this tea was produced and sold across the café this boosted the sales of the evaporated milk.

In the quest of culture preservation, Jobs have been created, service providers engaged, and profits realised, this is giving back to the society positively with earnings attached. It could be described as business initiatives that would continue with time and is bound to be modified for it to be more effective.

Case study 2, Healthier Kids programme handled by Nestle hong kong as a result of the growing population of obese and malnourished children, the focus was to ensure that healthier eating habit and proper physical activity are adapted. The campaign was taken to schools. The program involved the Centre for Health Education and Health Promotion (CHEP) of The Chinese University of Hong Kong, sessions were organised and relevant data collected from 6 primary schools in 3 years. This programme impacted positively on society by improving the health of the children, enhanced nutritional value, highlighted the importance of exercise. The business impact for nestle is that they could realize the problems and need to improve the nutritional qualities of food products that they produce.

Case study 3 is about Micro-franchised agricultural service expansion project Cambodia. The issue is an age-long one that involves, farming communities must rely on the land to survive. Without the help of modern agricultural techniques, quality inputs, up to date training and market linkages, farmers end up in poverty and they can barely provide for their families. Farm Business Advisor Model was adopted, world vision partnered with IDE and Lors Thmey. Farm business advisors were recruited locally and trained by Lors Thmey, their functions are to help the farmers improve their yields by selling agricultural inputs, provide farmers with technical supports to increase their production yields, creating economic value in the value chain. The project was very effective, 180 farmers sold their products to Lors Thmey and advisors pushed the products to the open market. This indicates that the farmers earned more revenue compared to the past when products rot because of inability to access the market.

They have produced a total 1,039 tonnes of cucumber, wax gourd and long bean, bitter gourd, chilli, eggplant, sweet pepper, water spinach and mustard greens, generating US$ 228,156 in revenue for farmers. A win-win situation for smallholder farmers, Farm Business Advisors and Lors Thmey as the techniques improved production and market connections also led to earnings unlike in the past.

Exploring Shared Value

Case study 4 looks at the shared value in Banking, Bendigo & Adelaide Bank, an Australian bank saw the opportunity in the Ageing Australian population mortgage loan repayment affects their cash flow and thereby reducing the quality of life at retirement. A new product was introduced called Homesafe wealth release® introduced in 2005, it allows the homeowner access to equity release on the property while the facility runs, and improved cash flow for the homeowner and continues to occupy the property. Homesafe facilitates the deferred sale of an agreed proportion of the family home. The homeowner sells a percentage of the future sale proceeds of their home in return for an immediate lump sum cash payment of up to $1 million.

The bank continues to receive enquiries about the product. As of December 2017, the fair value of the portfolio was $709.8m. Homesafe is a great example of a successfully shared value business model providing solid returns and great social outcomes. However, it has been a challenge to attract new funding partners. Funding will be required to make this product available to more senior Australian citizens, more partners would be required. Income earned by the bank and Ageing population adequately taken care of.

Case Study 5, Supporting clients, colleagues and communities to rise, an initiative of Barclays bank Hong Kong. Through its Social Innovation Facility (SIF), Barclays encourages colleagues to submit ideas that have commercial value whilst also solving pressing societal challenges. These ideas have been funded and integrated into the business of the bank. ideas for a new product or service that could also have a positive impact on society is submitted by employees of the institution for review, approval and adoption. About 50 social impact business ventures across the globe have been funded by Barclays' SIF. In some cases, employees have even created new internal opportunities for themselves in the organisation that have impacted them positively in terms of experience.

After six years SIF Banking group was established with the sole aim of providing support, such as sustainable agriculture, recycling, energy storage, electric transportation and financial services. A second focus of the group is building relationships with sustainability-focused investors across asset classes to better understand their needs and connect them with potential investments. The company is a firm believer that shared value programmes should be encouraged, no matter what the industry. "Things are changing so fast because of technology," The bank made profits by turning ideas into ventures, provide funding and Technical support for the promoters of this business and the impact derived cuts across some continents of the world, social problems turned to profit and we can see because it's an integral of the business, innovations with respect to its improvements continued and in the nearest future, it can become a whole bank subsidiary.

Case Study 5, Supporting clients, colleagues and communities to rise, an initiative of Barclays bank Hong Kong. Through its Social Innovation Facility (SIF), Barclays encourages colleagues to submit ideas that have commercial value whilst also solving pressing societal challenges. These ideas have been funded and integrated into the business of the bank. ideas for a new product or service that could also have a positive impact on society is submitted by employees of the institution for review, approval and adoption. About 50 social impact business ventures across the globe have been funded by Barclays' SIF. In some cases, employees have even created new internal opportunities for themselves in the organisation that have impacted them positively in terms of experience.

After six years SIF Banking group was established with the sole aim of providing support, such as sustainable agriculture, recycling, energy storage, electric transportation and financial services. A second focus of the group is building relationships with sustainability-focused investors across asset classes to better understand their needs and connect them with potential investments. The company is a firm believer that shared value programmes should be encouraged, no matter what the industry. "Things are changing so fast because of technology," The bank made profits by turning ideas into ventures, provide funding and Technical support for the promoters of this business and the impact derived cuts across some continents of the world, social problems turned to profit and we can see because it's an integral of the business, innovations with respect to its improvements continued and in the nearest future, it can become a whole bank subsidiary.

Case Study 6: SHARED VALUE IN LIFE INSURANCE, AIA Australia is an independent life insurance specialist with over 40 years of experience building successful partnerships and they found opportunities in this challenge in the society, Two in three Australians are currently overweight or obese and chronic disease is the leading cause of death and disability in the country and this has an effect on all sectors in Australia, including the life insurance industry. A reduction of this problem becomes paramount, improving the health of policyholders is the focus of AIA Australia. They launched Vitality, the world's leading health and wellness program, with more than 3.4 million members worldwide, the program is sold to subscribers of the life insurance policy.

Members begin the program by completing health and fitness assessments and earn points for undertaking healthy activities, such as running and going to the gym. In addition, members are rewarded with points for displaying healthy behaviour, including discounts on shopping, entertainment and travel purchases and discounts on their insurance premiums. This stimulates the subscribers since they are aware that they will receive rebates when they are actively involved in physical exercises, this improves their health and more so discounts would accrue on their premiums, shopping. The incentive becomes the bait for healthy living of the population and workforce remain efficient rather than embarking on sick leave that would impact negatively on the economy.

Case Study 7: Smart Power for Rural Development, Creating a Sustainable Market Solution to Energy Poverty. Providing electricity to the rural communities at a reduced cost. Rockefeller Foundation is supporting ESCOs* such as OMC, DESI Power, Tara Urja, and others to create shared value through its Smart Power for Rural Development Initiative. Shared value is a management approach that enables companies to increase profits, reduce costs, and enhance competitiveness by solving social problems, such as limited access to electricity. Rockefeller's Smart Power for Rural Development Initiative provides affordable financing to ESCOs and links them to an ecosystem of Rockefeller grant-funded partners.

Indian national government recognizes the lack of access to electricity as a social concern, and there are programs in place to extend grids in rural areas where access to electricity is the lowest.

Lack of access to reliable electricity has a negative impact on social and economic development, limiting people's ability to enhance their incomes, improve their health, increase their food security, educate their children, and access key information services. This was the opportunity identified by promoters of mini power firms. It will take communities about two decades to be connected to the national grid.

Rockefeller's main policy partner, Shakti Sustainable Energy Foundation, helps inform policies and regulations in India that impact the growth of the mini-grid market. providing financing through program-related investments (PRIs). A pioneer, the Foundation has been making PRIs—investments expected to generate both social impact and a concessionary financial return—since the 1990s. In the case of Smart Power India, Rockefeller is investing approximately $23 million in PRIs. The use of proceeds for the PRIs is to partially finance the capital expenditures incurred by the ESCOs when building plants.

OMC's partnership with the Rockefeller Foundation and Smart Power India enables OMC to quickly deepen relationships with rural businesses and local communities in order to connect rural consumers in a cost-efficient manner. The partnership of Rockefeller foundations with the Renewable energy firms led to the provision of power to the rural communities at an effective cost that is affordable thereby ensuring rural businesses save significant money on monthly energy expenditures, resulting in

Exploring Shared Value

increased income and business expansion. Though the model is still evolving considering challenges experienced with the cost of setting up the plant.

Exploring Shared Value

Chapter 4

Embracing this concept in Africa

There is an urgent need to embrace this concept in Africa by corporate entities operating in this continent, the focus should be on the rural areas, there is little that governments of these countries can achieve. Considering the features of this concept, challenges can be turned to profits.

Apart from rural communities, Africa is an emerging market for the rest of the world, corporate bodies should look inwards and take a deep study of the market, visualize opportunities that abound.

Agriculture is one area that requires attention, issues like **processing**, **preservation** of their produce, **adopting technologies** that would improve the yields of the commodities and most importantly creating a value chain that ensures effective sale of commodities in the cities. Some other issues like infrastructures Gap in such communities should be improved and I will give some valid examples.

In Nigeria, Rice production has taken an upward swing but faced with some challenges, this attribute for the reason why locally produced rice is as expensive as imported Thailand rice. Issues like increasing the yields by educating the farmers, Machinery for processing, availability cheap funding to all the farmers etc. Government efforts should be commended, the private sector can get involved by providing services for profit, the Cambodian case study is an example that should be replicated.

It would make sense for Africans to be part of Shared initiative Africa, become members and attend seminars organised, this will not only help in boosting ideas but also expose models executed by corporations for adoption with little modifications in our countries.

One critical issue is power, infrastructures like Roads, bridges etc. are areas that must be considered for shared value initiatives.

Exploring Shared Value

Governments should not be the only ones involved in infrastructure development alone but could serve as an enabler for the private sector that wants to embark on such shared value initiatives.

The government can play the role of an enabler with respect to infrastructure maintenance, provision by corporate bodies giving rebates with respect to tax rebates for such organisations.

I have come across accidental Shared value initiates done by some corporations in Nigeria, 'Dangote building over 100Km road with cement', I'm not very sure of the arrangement it reached with government with respect to this project, it might just be an avenue for them to sell the idea so as to substitute coal tar that makes road construction very expensive, the word accidental was used to stress that it was just a CSR initiative.

Tony Elumelu foundation providing funds for farmers in Benue state, the food basket of the nation. In 2011, we invested in agriculture in Benue State [Nigeria], which is considered the food basket of the nation. This is a part of the country that yields a significant amount of Nigeria's produce, including citrus fruits. Yet, despite the high demand for fruit juice, Benue had never successfully established the capacity to convert the raw produce to a consumer product that had a ready market. In the meantime, Nigeria continued importing tons of fruit juice concentrate to serve the growing middle-class population. We invested in a local juice concentrate plant supplying makers of fruit juice, which is the first of its kind in Nigeria, and this is already having a positive and measurable impact on the community. We purchase oranges, pineapples and mangoes that previously couldn't be sold and would be left to rot on the ground—as much as 60% of the production was lost every year. We're empowering the community, from farmers to the many that are directly and indirectly employed by our activities, and we've introduced technology to the country that hitherto never existed—that to us is truly shared value.

(Tony Elumelu: Shared Value Synonymous with Africapitalism, By: Michelle Morgan, Senior Manager, Communications at Shared Value Initiative April 15th, 2014)

Lafarge cement program on Agricultural Ecology Intervention In agrarian communities like those in Gombe State, agricultural transformation is crucial to ensuring an improved socio-economic landscape and overall standard of living for residents of the community.

This transformation has huge potentials to bring about poverty reduction,

improved nutrition, and food security. In line with this, Lafarge Africa Plc.,

through its subsidiary; Ashaka Cement, launched the "Agricultural Ecology

Intervention" in 2017. This initiative presents us with an opportunity to support the Nigerian government in addressing the interlinked challenges

of poverty, food security and climate change.

The Agricultural Ecology Intervention is executed in collaboration with

agriculture experts and the National Agricultural Extension and Research

Liaison Services (NAERLS) in Ahmadu Bello University, Zaria. Other

important stakeholders are collaborating on this initiative are the Ministry

of Agriculture, local government authorities, emirs and community

leaders, as well as farmers' associations. The following are the specific support structures and practices which we have instituted for benefitting smallholder farmers:

• Capacity building training

Exploring Shared Value

- Support in adopting agricultural innovations and more efficient

  agricultural practices

- Support with fertile land for farming

- Real-time expert guidance for farmers through the planting cycle

- Business support and guidance to ensure profitability for farmers

Primarily, we empower small scale farmers with required skills, resources

and technical support that helps foster increased productivity and

economic yields. With the results, we have seen within our first year

of operation, we believe that the ripple effect of this intervention on

the socio-economic landscape of the benefitting communities will be astounding. The Agricultural Ecology Intervention has led to higher productivity for benefiting farmers and the following are some

of the successes recorded in 2018. Improved agricultural yields and more profits for benefitting farmers Training Seed usage optimization Fertilizer use

Greenhouse Farming1 Agricultural Innovation

• Across 7 villages, we trained 600 farmers on best practices in seed

    selection, planting techniques and crop-mixing for bio-pest control.

• These villages are - Bajoga; Lariski, Darumpa, Malari.; Ashaka Gari

    war kungiya; Badabdi Village; Jalingo Ashaka; Gongila and Juggol;

    and Bage Village.

• In 2018, we recorded a 30% reduction in seed usage, based on new planting techniques.

• 40% reduction in fertilizer usage as a result of smarter farming methods

• Greenhouse farming systems were introduced to help farmers minimise

the risk of pest attacks

• We successfully deployed the 'three-season' farming system, which

ensures that benefitting farmers have yielded all year round

• Two new crops introduced (Irish potatoes and sesame)

• We supported farmers with the introduction of high plant varieties like –

maize, tomatoes, and sorghum.

(Shared Value for Sustained Growth, Lafarge Cement, 2018 Report)

We must commend Lafarge for providing technical support for the farmers, a critical look at this report shows that it's purely a CSR initiative. It is commendable for their interest in rural communities.

Our financial institutions(FI) should come alive in their responsibilities by taking a cue from the Barclays bank Hong Kong model that turns an idea conceived in solving societal problems to profit with innovations, our FI's are only interested in quick earnings, I remember the underground rail station from London to Paris underneath water, this project was financed by a bank in the united kingdom through the arrangement was BOT – Build, Operate and transfer. This would facilitate the recovery of their initial investments on the project, this example is not a shared value initiative but to prove that our FI's in Africa can be more responsible than they are now.

Efforts should be directed on improving our continent, wealth creation and above all corporations should be innovative, visualize opportunities that are staring us in the face.

Exploring Shared Value

Our emphasis has been on corporate bodies, public sector and governments should be involved in this golden initiative. An example is BRICS formed by five countries – Brazil, Russia, India, China and South Africa. The aim was cooperation among these countries in terms of trade, technology and bilateral agreements that will lift and improve lives in their countries. China is at the centre because of its advancements in production and exporting products all over the world. Can you imagine Russia and China connected via Road, these countries embarked on this project jointly to ease the movement of goods by road, an expensive project that has a positive effect on the long run.

Budgets in most African countries are usually one-sided, recurrent expenditure has the highest allocation, other sectors don't have enough to carry out their projects, funding the budget is a major headache for these African states. The public institutions should be made to generate their funds and relief the governments of the stress of funding their recurrent expenditures. This institution should embrace the shared value initiative, the implication is that the institution will become stronger and relevant in terms of resolving societal problems and making earnings from it.

Corporations should embrace this concept by integrating it into their business model, this will not only solve societal issues but also improve their earnings and touch lives positively. Government must be involved in such initiative and multinationals to make it more robust and effective.

A few years ago, Mars was faced with the realization that we needed another Côte d'Ivoire to produce enough cocoa to meet the world's growing chocolate demand by 2020. Given that cocoa was becoming a less attractive crop for farmers, and that Côte d'Ivoire was in a cycle of decline, we knew we needed a strategy for cocoa sustainability. As a company that's always had a commitment to the people and

Exploring Shared Value

communities in which we work, we also wanted to ensure that farmers would benefit. We worked with FSG on a shared value strategy to ensure the long-term success of our chocolate business while improving the conditions for farmers.

(Shared Value in Côte D'Ivoire, Creating a Vibrant Cocoa Sector, FSG)

Exploring Shared Value

About the Author

Alexander Abiodun Ndukwe, born 5th January 1971 at Ebutte Metta Lagos by Late Chief Ndukwe Agwu and Mrs Theresa Agwu, they hail from Amaokwe Item, Bende Local government, Abia State.

Alex attended Lantana Private School and St. Saviour Primary School, Obanikoro where he obtained his First School Leaving Certificate in 1982. He proceeded to Baptist Academy Secondary School, Obanikoro in 1983 and he obtained West African School Certificate Examination (WASCE) in 1988.

He gained Admission to study Computer science at the University of Nigeria Nsukka in 1989/90 session, he bagged Bachelor of Science degree in Computer Science with a Second-Class Lower Division in 1994.

Completed National Youth Service Corps in Lagos state in 1995, had his primary assignment

Exploring Shared Value

at Union Bank Data Centre, Research & Development unit, Aerodrome Road, Apapa.

September 1995, he got a Job at Indo-Nigerian Merchant Bank Limited as Analyst/Programmer at the Head office situated at 42 Adeola Hopewell, Victoria Island, Lagos and December 27th, 1995 Alex was transferred to Kano to handle Information Technology Unit of the branch.

December 1998 Alex gave his life to Christ at the Redeemed Christian church of God, Victory Parish and joined the workforce in 1999 and was transferred to Solid Rock Parish as an Usher, this was on a part-time basis as his circular Job continued. September 2nd, 2000 Alex got married to Adaku Chigbu and the union is blessed with 3 children, Deborah, David and Daniel.

Alex continued to make progress in his circular Job while fully involved in working for God in his vineyard, in 2002 Alex rose to the rank of Assistant Manager (Information Technology) at Indo-Nigeria Bank. He had also commenced his

Master's in Business Administration at Ambrose Alli University Ekpoma in the preceding year and the programme was completed in November 2004.

In August 2005, Alex was ordained Deacon at the Redeemed Christian Church of God, during the Let's Go A Fishing programme of November 2005, Alex was appointed Parish Pastor, Goshen Sanctuary which was planted by the Area Pastor of Solid Rock, Area Pastor, Sola Ayindiji. The same year Indo-Nigerian Bank Limited merged with four other banks to form a new bank called Sterling Bank Plc, which commenced operations 2nd January 2006.

The Merger came with pains, employees from Indo-Nigerian Bank were demoted by one step and the enumeration was higher by over 300 per cent, some of my colleagues resigned but I continued, and the Lord remained faithful.

The Bank became bigger, Alex had to cover North-west Region which was made up of Kano with 7 branches and deployment of Technology Infrastructure to new locations like Gusau, Sokoto, Katsina, Dutse and Maiduguri and these locations commenced operations and Technology issues were managed by Alex.

In 2007 Pastor Alex was transferred to RCCG, Open doors Parish as Parish pastor during the reconfiguration of the province that was done by the Regional pastor, Special Assistant to General Overseer, Pastor Remi Akintunde and after 3 months Pastor Alex was transferred to Trinity Area Headquarters as Area Pastor and the Lord was indeed faithful, Alex Planted 7 Parishes. In 2008 Alex was transferred to Gateway zone and became Zonal Pastor, the Lord remained faithful and Alex planted 9 parishes at this zone, he had a slogan, 'Go-A-Fishing without planting a parish is a waste of Resources'. 2010 Alex was ordained, Assistant Pastor. He was transferred to Ambassadors Zone as Zonal Pastor.

Alex continued to make progress in the circular as he rose to the rank of Deputy Manager in

2010, he continued to manage ICT infrastructures and the ATM's were deployed across the branches and in October 2014 he was transferred to FCT as Clustered Head Support(North) managing 42 Northern branches of Sterling bank. Alex was promoted Manager in 2015. In 2016 Alex left the services of the bank and floated an ICT firm called TEKVILLE SYSTEMS.

In 2018 Alex completed his doctorate degree in computer science at Atlantic International University, Florida, United States.

References

Shared Value Initiative Interview with Rohit Chandra, Managing Director and Co-Founder, OMC Power, September 3rd, 2015 (via phone).

2 "Fortune India: Light club – India's solar entrepreneurs." Hindol Sengupta. Fortune India. July 2015. http://www.omcpower.com/blog/p/

fortune-India-light-club-indias-solar-entrepreneurs.

3 "Fortune India: Light club – India's solar entrepreneurs." Sengupta, Hindol. Fortune India. July 2015. http://www.omcpower.com/blog/p/

fortune-India-light-club-indias-solar-entrepreneurs.

4 Shared Value Initiative Interview with Rohit Chandra, Managing Director and Co-Founder, OMC Power. September 3rd, 2015 (via phone).

5 Shared Value Initiative Interview with Rohit Chandra, Managing Director and Co-Founder, OMC Power. September 3rd, 2015 (via phone).

6 Shared Value Initiative Interview with Rohit Chandra, Managing Director and Co-Founder, OMC Power. September 3rd, 2015 (via phone).

7 Shared Value Initiative Interview with Rohit Chandra, Managing Director and Co-Founder, OMC Power. September 3rd, 2015 (via phone).

8 "Fortune India: Light club – India's solar entrepreneurs." Hindol Sengupta. Fortune India. July 2015. http://www.omcpower.com/blog/p/

fortune-India-light-club-indias-solar-entrepreneurs.

9 Shared Value Initiative Interview with Rohit Chandra, Managing Director and Co-Founder, OMC Power. September 3rd, 2015 (via phone).

10 Shared Value Initiative Interview with Rohit Chandra, Managing Director and Co-Founder, OMC Power. September 3rd, 2015 (via phone).

11 Shared Value Initiative Interview with Rohit Chandra, Managing Director and Co-Founder, OMC Power. September 3rd, 2015 (via phone).

12 "Sustainable Energy for All (SE4ALL)- Electricity Access Fact Sheet" United Nations. http://www.se4all.org/sites/default/files/l/2013/09/

EnergyAccess.pdf.

13 "Sustainable Energy for All (SE4ALL)- Electricity Access Fact Sheet" United Nations.http://www.se4all.org/sites/default/files/l/2013/09/

EnergyAccess.pdf.

14 World Energy Outlook 2014 Database. International Energy Agency. http://www.worldenergyoutlook.org/resources/energydevelopment/

energyaccessdatabase/#d.en.8609.

15 World Energy Outlook 2014 Database. International Energy Agency. http://www.worldenergyoutlook.org/resources/energydevelopment/

energyaccessdatabase/#d.en.8609.

16 The Rockefeller Foundation Smart Power for Rural Development Initiative Analysis. Supplement for June 2014 Board Discussion.

17 "Decentralized Electricity in Africa and Southeast Asia." Ashvin Dayal, Accenture Development Partnerships. January 2015. https://www.

rockefellerfoundation.org/report/de-centralized-electricity-in-africa-and-southeast-asia/.

18 "The Business Case for Off-Grid Energy in India." The Climate Group in partnership with Goldman Sachs Center for Environmental Markets.2014. http://global-off-grid-lighting-association.org/wp-content/uploads/2015/05/The-business-case-for-offgrid-energy-in-India.pdf.

19 "Decentralized Electricity in Africa and Southeast Asia." Ashvin Dayal, Accenture Development Partnerships. January 2015. https://www.

Exploring Shared Value

rockefellerfoundation.org/report/de-centralized-electricity-in-africa-and-southeast-asia/.

20 "Decentralized Electricity in Africa and Southeast Asia." Ashvin Dayal, Accenture Development Partnerships. January 2015. https://www.

rockefellerfoundation.org/report/de-centralized-electricity-in-africa-and-southeast-asia/.

21 "Decentralized Electricity in Africa and Southeast Asia." Ashvin Dayal, Accenture Development Partnerships. January 2015. https://www.rockefellerfoundation.org/report/de-centralized-electricity-in-africa-and-southeast-asia/.

22 "The Business Case for Off-Grid Energy in India." The Climate Group in partnership with Goldman Sachs Center for Environmental Markets. 2014. http://global-off-grid-lighting-association.org/wp-content/uploads/2015/05/The-business-case-for-offgrid-energy-in-India.pdf.

23 Shared Value Initiative Interview with Jaideep Mukherji, CEO, Smart Power India. September 18th, 2015 (via phone).

24 "The Business Case for Off-Grid Energy in India." The Climate Group in partnership with Goldman Sachs Center for Environmental Markets.

2014.http://global-off-grid-lighting-association.org/wp-content/uploads/2015/05/The-business-case-for-offgrid-energy-in-India.pdf.

25 "Energy for the Telecom Towers India Market Sizing and Forecasting, IFC." GSMA and IFC. 2011. http://www.gsma.com/mobilefordevelopment/wp-content/uploads/2012/05/Energy-for-the-Telecom-Towers-India-Market-Sizing-and-ForecastingSeptember-2010.pdf.

26 Shared Value Initiative Interview with Shrihari Kulkarni, Chief Financial Officer, OMC Power. September 3rd, 2015 (via phone).

27 "Leveraging Telecom Towers to Address Energy Poverty in India." Smart Power for Rural Development, The Rockefeller Foundation.

February   2013.
https://www.rockefellerfoundation.org/report/leveraging-telecom-towers-to-address-energy-poverty-in-india/.

28 The Rockefeller Foundation Smart Power for Rural Development Initiative Analysis. Supplement for June 2014 Board Discussion.

29 "Beyond the Grid: Solar Power for Everyone." Pariphan Uawithya, Senior Program Associate, Rockefeller, November 2014. https://www.

rockefellerfoundation.org/blog/beyond-grid-solar-power-everyone/.

30 "The Business Case for Off-Grid Energy in India." The Climate Group in partnership with Goldman Sachs Centre for Environmental Markets.2014.   http://global-off-grid-lighting-association.org/wp-

content/uploads/2015/05/The-business-case-for-offgrid-energy-in-India.pdf.

31 "The Business Case for Off-Grid Energy in India." The Climate Group in partnership with Goldman Sachs Centre for Environmental Markets.2014.http://global-off-grid-lighting-association.org/wp-content/uploads/2015/05/The-business-case-for-offgrid-energy-in-India.pdf.

32 The Rockefeller Foundation Smart Power for Rural Development Initiative Analysis. Supplement for June 2014 Board Discussion.

33 The Rockefeller Foundation Smart Power for Rural Development Initiative Analysis. Supplement for June 2014 Board Discussion.

34 See Beyond the Pioneer: Getting Inclusive Businesses to Scale. Harvey Koh, et al. Monitor Inclusive Markets, Deloitte. 2014. http://www.

beyondthepioneer.org/beyond-the-pioneer-report.

35 Shared Value Initiative Interview with Pooja Raman, Legal Counsel and Investment Lead, OMC Power, September 3rd, 2015 (via phone).

36 The Rockefeller Foundation Smart Power for Rural Development Initiative Analysis. Supplement for June 2014 Board Discussion.

37 The Rockefeller Foundation Smart Power for Rural Development Initiative Analysis. Supplement for June 2014 Board Discussion.

38 The Rockefeller Foundation Smart Power for Rural Development Initiative Analysis. Supplement for June 2014 Board Discussion.

39 The Rockefeller Foundation Smart Power for Rural Development Initiative Analysis. Smart Power Business Model Refresh. 2015.

40 The Rockefeller Foundation Smart Power for Rural Development Initiative Analysis. Supplement for June 2014 Board Discussion.

41 Shared Value Initiative Interview with Pooja Raman, Legal Counsel and Investment Lead, OMC Power, September 3rd, 2015 (via phone).

42 Shared Value Interview with Sanjay Khazanci, Independent Consultant. September 14th, 2015 (via phone).

43 Shared Value Initiative e-mail exchange with Clare Boland Ross, Associate Director, Rockefeller Foundation. September 16th, 2015.

44 "Leveraging Telecom Towers to Address Energy Poverty in India." Smart Power for Rural Development, The Rockefeller Foundation. February 2013. https://www.rockefellerfoundation.org/report/leveraging-telecom-towers-to-address-energy-poverty-in-india/.

45 Shared Value Initiative Interview with Deepak Gupta, Senior Program Manager (Power), Shakti Sustainable Energy Foundation, September 9th, 2015 (via phone).

46 Shared Value Initiative Interview with Deepak Gupta, Senior Program Manager (Power), Shakti Sustainable Energy Foundation, September 9th, 2015 (via phone).

47 Shared Value Initiative Interview with Jaideep Mukherji, CEO, Smart Power India. September 18th, 2015 (via phone).

48 The Rockefeller Foundation Smart Power for Rural Development Initiative Monitoring and Evaluation Review.

49 Findings from Smart Power for Rural Development Monitoring Round 1. Self-reported data from ESCOs collected and compiled by

Accenture Development Partners/ Smart Power India through SIMS. Additional analysis from Dalberg Global Development Advisors and

Sambodhi. 2015. 50 Shared Value Initiative Interview with Pariphan Uawithya, Sr. Program Associate, Rockefeller Foundation. September 24th, 2015.

51 Findings from Smart Power for Rural Development Monitoring Round 1. Self-reported data from ESCOs collected and compiled by

Accenture Development Partners/ Smart Power India through SIMS. Additional analysis from Dalberg Global Development Advisors and

Sambodhi. 2015.

52 Smart Power for Rural Development Early Impact Document, June/July 2015. Sent via e-mail by Pariphan Uawithya, Sr. Program Associate,

Rockefeller Foundation. September 24th, 2015.

53 Findings from Smart Power for Rural Development Monitoring Round 1. Self-reported data from ESCOs collected and compiled by

Accenture Development Partners/ Smart Power India through SIMS. Additional analysis from Dalberg Global Development Advisors and

Sambodhi. 2015.

54 The Rockefeller Foundation Smart Power for Rural Development Initiative Analysis. Supplement for June 2014 Board Discussion.

55 Findings from Smart Power for Rural Development Monitoring Round 1. Self-reported data from ESCOs collected and compiled by

Accenture Development Partners/ Smart Power India through SIMS. Additional analysis from Dalberg Global Development Advisors and

Sambodhi. 2015.

56 Shared Value Initiative Interview with Jaideep Mukherji, CEO, Smart Power India. September 18th, 2015 (via phone).

57 Shared Value Initiative Interview with Jaideep Mukherji, CEO, Smart Power India. September 18th, 2015 (via phone).

www.ingramcontent.com/pod-product-compliance
Lightning Source LLC
Chambersburg PA
CBHW022040190326
41520CB00008B/661